From DEADWOOD to Diamonds

STEFAN KAZAKIS

First published in 2014 by Major Street Publishing Pty Ltd
PO Box 106, Highett, Vic. 3190.
Contact: info@majorstreet.com.au

National Library of Australia Cataloguing-in-Publication data:

Author:	Kazakis, Stefan, author.
Title:	From deadwood to diamonds: how small business owners can come back from the brink and achieve big business success / Stefan Kazakis.
ISBN:	9780987542939 (paperback)
Subjects:	Small business--Australia.
	Success in business--Australia.
	Entrepreneurship--Australia.
Dewey Number:	658.0220994

Cover design by Pipeline Design
Internal design by Production Works
Printed in Australia by Griffin Press

10 9 8 7 6 5 4 3 2 1

READ WHAT CLIENTS SAY ABOUT STEFAN KAZAKIS

Slowly… things are starting to congeal for me. I am learning slowly and it is sinking in.

On a personal note, I think it is necessary to let you know the difference you have made to me. Frankly, I don't know where I would be without your guidance – probably, unemployed and bankrupt. Thank you for showing me how to seek clarity and how to "dig deep". I do have a way to go yet… however, I know I am going to get there if I keep listening to and practising what you preach. A lot of what you teach is not just about business but about integrity and it can be instilled into our family values. In case you ever second-guess what you are doing with Board of Directors 12…please come back to this message. You have saved my family. I am indebted. Thank you so much.

—Paul Kite, Main Street Music

We were getting complacent and caught up in the day-to-day running of our businesses, and we struggled with clarity and direction.

We will never look back! Stefan has helped us greatly with clarity over our business, and our future direction. Last year we had three gyms, as well as three other peripheral businesses in completely different industries, largely to satisfy Ben's entrepreneurial spirit, but also due to a lack of strategic direction on our behalf. We are now getting out of the outside three to focus on our core business of the health clubs. Our new mantra is – 'do one thing and do it well'! We have redefined our own responsibilities so that we are no longer stepping on each other's toes. It has also eliminated the confusion our team had with who to report to or who to contact. The way we work together now as business partners, and husband and wife, is incomparable to the past two years. No more tears or arguments. We are on the same page every day, we share common goals, and in a way, our coaching sessions are somewhat like counselling sessions!

The future is exciting and we are pumped to pursue it. Not only are we excited, but we are confident in our continued success, and in achieving not only our business goals but our life goals as well. Stefan stresses the importance of celebrating our successes. And with his support and coaching, we are confident we will continue, if not exceed, our goal of 40% profit growth this financial year.

We would wholeheartedly recommend Stefan to any business owner who is open to change and wants to be successful, no matter their end goal.

—Emma and Ben Stallworthy, Pinnacle Health Clubs

Tom and I have been asking the questions, what can't we see? What don't we know? What's the worst case scenario and Plan B? We feel we have turned a potential disaster into a significant growth opportunity.

P.S. Thank you! Tom and I feel that we have been able to deal with this situation so much better than we would have done before Board of Directors 12 and the workshops. The learning over the last eight months has been so valuable, and

it shows it in times like these. We're definitely not counting
our chickens before they hatch but we are looking forward
to continuing with our strategy and not falling back into old
habits just to survive.

—Doug and Tom Graham, Tough Glass Works

Stefan is a passionate, engaging and insightful business coach
who has made a considerable contribution to the development
of our management team. He challenges us continuously to
ensure we hold ourselves accountable and look at things
from a different perspective.

—Cameron Brookes, Kiandra IT

Before working with Stefan, I had no time to myself,
working 24/7. Now I'm organised with my weekends off. We
have grown in leaps and bounds. If that's what Stefan can do
in seven sessions, I'm afraid of letting the reins go in the
business and see how far we can go…

—David Lindsay, Salts of the Earth

You can spend hours, and thousands [of dollars] on seminars
and courses getting to the same conclusions. High intensity
and fast-pace allowed the most important strategies to
impact bottom line profits to come to the surface.

—Tina Robertson, Asenz

ACKNOWLEDGMENTS

There are many people I wish to thank for their contribution to this book. The list is so long that to name them all would require a further 50 pages. They have influenced me in so many ways and have made my journey to this point phenomenal.

Gratitude to all my mentors, specifically Mum, Dad, Basil, Brad and Keith, and to all my clients who shaped my journey thus far, and to the many others who believe in me and give me the power of words and resilience to continue on my rewarding road of influencing small business owners to grow their diamonds and excel their quality of life continuously. You are the best!

On a personal note I wish to thank my beautiful wife of almost 20 years, Terri. You are our rock and I thank you. There is no better place for a business owner than to be at home at the kitchen table every night being supported by loved ones.

And to my amazing two boys Stephen and Harris, your journey in life and the role model I choose to be for you at every step is the greatest and most fulfilling challenge for me as an influence of everything that is possible in life. It's your progress as meaningful citizens in the world that fuels the fire in my belly more than anything else.

I wish to also thank my team on this project: Nikki Sadler, Michael Hanrahan and Lesley Williams. Their strengths 'in writing flowing English' combined with my strengths to make the 'challenging somewhat easy' make this book a transformational read for all business owners at all levels.

And finally to you as the reader – the current and future business leader of a diamond that will make a difference to your chosen team, customer and community that you will build and influence with your solutions to their problems.

Gratitude and Power to You!

This is a book for business owners who just know they are on the way to something amazing, something that will make a difference. This is a book about 'walking the talk', about the journey of business and what it takes to get the breakthrough you deserve, regardless of your level or size. We are often at a crossroads that requires us to make a decision to move from deadwood to diamond…

It is my deepest intent to serve you and inspire you to become the diamond you deserve to be.

CONTENTS

PREFACE: YOU ARE SITTING ON A DIAMOND

There are thousands of small business-owners around Australia right now, running a micro business from the kitchen table or managing small teams of employees in a bigger (small) business. Most of the time they think they are successful. When they are asked, 'How's the business going?', they respond, 'Yeah, okay. Could be better, but paying the bills.'

If they are really honest with themselves, though, they would admit that the 'success' they are achieving falls a little short of the expectations they had for the business when they started out. They have been working hard and have made something out of a really good opportunity, but retirement is looming, their super is not enough to enjoy a comfortable retirement and – more of a worry – their health's not great either. Their health is suffering because even if the business is going 'okay', their work/life situation is not in harmony. One of the original drivers to work for themselves – to have more control in their personal life – has not been achieved. In fact, when things aren't going well most small business owners end up working many more hours than they would in regular employment, often for less money.

I've seen this happen time and time again. The other thing I've seen time and time again is a sense of hopelessness at this point. These business owners are smart and they work hard – that's certainly not the problem – but they just can't figure out why they are not getting ahead. At some point they realise that what's missing is education. They need somebody to point them in the right direction and walk next to them while they get back on track or advance the track they are on.

That's when they come to me.

A central theme of everything I do is **Brutal Truth**. I'm going to explain this to you right here, because it's essential that you take this approach if you want to turn your business around. It is absolutely non-negotiable that you are 100% brutally honest with yourself while you are trying to transform your business. Not 73%. Not 96%. You need 100%. Get it? All the education and information in the world will not help you if you don't have this mindset. In *From Deadwood to Diamonds* you will find all sorts of wonderful formulas, techniques, tools, systems and tips that will turn your business around *if you apply them with honesty and determination*. I can teach you what to do but I can't do it for you; the courage and motivation to change your life has to come from you, and this comes from looking at your situation with Brutal Truth.

If you are not prepared to accept and deal with what you need to do in your business with honesty and determination, your business is going nowhere. And if your business is going nowhere it is in fact going *backwards* because in business there are only two directions: forwards and backwards. There is no in between.

So, it's time for a Brutal Truth moment: is your business deadwood, or on the way to being deadwood? You may not have thought about this before, so think about it now. Or maybe it's obvious. Perhaps you bought this book with the last money in your bank account (smart move). Maybe the electricity has already been turned off. Maybe you've been using the bathroom window to come and go because debt collectors are sitting on your doorstep. Maybe it's the Tax Office that's chasing you – and they are relentless. Even if it's not this obvious, you must make an assessment. Is your business deadwood?

You may have trouble accepting this about your business. It's an unsettling thought. I'd like to get all warm and fuzzy and say everything is going to be okay and pat you on the shoulder and say I understand – but that's not going to help you. If your business is deadwood the only way to remedy this is recognise it, to take responsibility for it, and commit to moving forward. No excuses. No more sitting around and saying, 'Hey, maybe next month will be better', because it won't be if you don't make it happen. Whatever state your business is in is your responsibility. But here's what's so great about that: this also gives you the power to change it.

Just as important as it is for you to accept your business is deadwood – or on its way there – is for you to recognise that you are truly sitting on a diamond. It just hasn't been discovered yet. I've worked with business owners who were literally days away from closing their doors, who well and truly knew they were deadwood and didn't know what to do about it. I've taken businesses from near-collapse to millions of dollars turnover a year. I've helped lost and confused owners realise their dreams. I've turned empty stores into thriving communities and quiet offices into profit-making powerhouses. So whatever stage you are at, recognise it, own it and accept it, but also recognise, own and accept that you can and will find a diamond if you are prepared to do what it takes.

At this moment of acceptance your work begins.

Are you prepared to do what it takes? I guess we're going to find out…

STEFAN KAZAKIS
Melbourne, 2014

INTRODUCTION: UNLOCKING YOUR PROFIT POTENTIAL

You've taken the first step by opening this book. Congratulations! You've made a start. This book will help you unlock the profit potential lurking in your business right now. We're going to look at finding clarity about what you are doing and why, how to build your business around this, how to identify and locate your ideal target market, how to manage the people side of things – in fact, this book contains everything you need to go from deadwood to diamonds.

Diamonds are graded into over 5,000 categories, and how they score in these categories determines their value. Your business is no different. There are many different aspects to making sustainable profits, and your business must score well in all of them if it's to have a strong future. We're going to examine your business on the basis of:

- clarity
- cut
- colour
- carat
- certification.

Clarity

The first part of this book helps business owners assess the clarity of their businesses. The more clarity you have, the more confidence you will have to move your business forward with purpose. The clarity of diamonds ranges from 'flawless' down to 'imperfect'. While a diamond's clarity cannot be improved, the good news is that business owners can add clarity to their vision and business plans.

Cut

The cut of a diamond is not simply its shape. The way a diamond is cut is primarily dependent upon the original shape of the rough stone, the location of the inclusions and the flaws that need to be eliminated. Cut is often regarded as the most important aspect of a diamond. In Part 2 of this book you will learn how to review the underlying foundation of your business and what you are shaping it for.

Colour

All natural diamonds contain small quantities of nitrogen atoms that affect the colouration, in the same way that the internal processes in your business create predictability for profitability. Part 3 of the book will show you how to work on improving your company's colour to retain customers and increase referrals.

Carat

A diamond's carat is a measurement of both the size and weight of the gemstone. One carat is equal to 0.2 grams. A carat can also be divided into 'points' with one carat being equal to 100 points, and with each point being 2 milligrams in weight. The size and depth of a small business is its 'carat'. In Part 4 we look at how you can add value to your business to make sure it has maximum carats. Conceptually, there is no limit to the weight of a diamond and therefore the number of carats – the bigger the diamond, the bigger the number of carats. In the same way, there is no limit to the heights your business can achieve.

Certification

Certification is how others see your business and provides the rubber stamp for what you do. It's a confirmation that what you are doing is genuine and authentic. It's worthwhile and it has value. It has been endorsed by your clients, suppliers and the team that are involved. How does your business rate? Are you building a base of raving fans who will help propel your business into the future?

The case studies

There is a case study at the end of each of these parts of the book. These are clients of mine who have achieved great success following the strategies you are about to read. They have businesses that are well-grounded, having a go and doing whatever it takes. There is great wisdom in these case studies, so I suggest you read and consider them carefully. Each case study covers many of the issues we'll be examining in the book, and each of these businesses is still in the process of evolution and growth – as successful businesses always are – because the journey never ends! You'll see how the application of these strategies is producing great results, and perhaps pick up a few tips that you can apply to your own business.

This is the five Cs in action.

Also, I've created two fictional characters – and I do mean fictional – Brendan and Danielle, and used them in examples of typical business owners facing some of the issues we are going to look at. These two characters are named in honour of two of my initial long-term clients, but they in no way actually represent these two wonderful business owners.

Part 1: Clarity

“ The critical ingredient is getting off your butt and doing something. It's as simple as that. A lot of people have ideas, but there are few who decide to do something about them now. Not tomorrow. Not next week, but today. The true entrepreneur is a doer, not a dreamer. ”

—Nolan Bushnell

The clarity of a diamond is assessed by its visual appearance. The more clarity it has, the more valuable it is – just like a business! Having clarity is all about knowing where you are going and why. It's about knowing who and where your customers are and why they buy from you. It's about finding the problems in your business and overcoming them.

1. IT ALL STARTS WITH CLARITY

Many years ago I was asked by a family member to manage an establishment in Mount Gambier. It was a hotel, and the tenants had been doing a lousy job. They were considerably behind on their rent and had run the property down, so there was no alternative but to evict them.

I was assigned to take control of this business until such time as the landlord was able to sell the freehold and the business (they told me no more than three months). I was in my early twenties and a novice 'businessman', but I took up the challenge as I was living between Australia and the Greek holiday island of Rhodes at the time, lacking a little direction.

I soon found out that the business was dead – it truly was 'deadwood'. Although I had worked in bars in Rhodes, I had never been officially involved in managing a business, and definitely not a business like this. I didn't even know how to butter toast when I arrived, but I was keen and energetic and within a couple of weeks I was making poached eggs on toast for the guests and getting paid for it.

At that tender age, in the early 1990s, in the remote South Australian town of Mount Gambier, I was all on my own managing a 'dead business'. I had no support, no-one to talk to and I felt as if I were in a dark, dark place. I still vividly remember the day when I punched a brick wall in frustration – to the point of drawing blood – and I still have the scars to remind me.

I refer to this period as my 'military service' and it was a turning point for all my entrepreneurial achievements. I managed to overcome my despair and find some clarity on what needed to be done to turn things around. This resulted in my forming a plan that assisted me in finding the strength to start the transformation of the business.

Within four weeks we had the restaurant and bar section of this establishment fully booked, every week, which greatly improved cashflow. I did this by hiring waitresses and bar staff who were considered the 'popular' girls in the town. They worked the floor and bar every night. At about 10 pm every night we would play 'Zorba the Greek' and get the patrons involved in some dancing and breaking of plates. It didn't take long before this restaurant run by a city boy became the talk of the town. It earned the reputation for being a place where you ate well, got great service and good old-fashioned Greek plate-breaking entertainment! Within just eight weeks this restaurant and bar were booked out weeks in advance as the establishment became relevant once again in the hearts and minds of the people of Mount Gambier.

I stayed there almost 12 months, and as much as the turnaround in the hotel was impressive, the turnaround in me was far more so. This experience would serve me for the rest of my life. I will never forget the initial despair and have never experienced it since.

The turning point in my story at Mount Gambier was when I found clarity. The choices I faced became clear. I saw where I needed to take the hotel and found a way to get there. The moral of my story is that in business and life we all face choices and the best way to make a choice is to be clear on where it will take you. What does this 'Point B' look like? How will you know when you get there? What are the first steps you need to take to start this journey? And most importantly, how far are you prepared to go to ensure you develop the discipline to achieve the transformation from Point A to Point B?

This is where the journey towards transforming the shape of your small business begins. Remember your business doesn't need to be the biggest or grandest, all it needs to be is a profitable business that will allow you to improve your quality of life, whatever that may mean to you.

ARE YOU REALLY READY FOR CHANGE?

If you're reading this book you've recognised the need for transformation in your business. Maybe you recognised it just yesterday or maybe it was six months ago, but you've now reached the point where you're ready to make something happen. You've had enough of working hard to pay off your overdue bills, of worrying that every client will be your last, of watching your bank account go into the red, of having to reintroduce yourself to your family when you bump into them on your one day off a month. You've decided it's time.

Haven't you?

You may *think* that you have, but to turn your deadwood into diamonds *thinking* that you're ready to change is not enough. You *have* to know more than anything that you are ready and willing to transform yourself and your business, that you are prepared to do what you have to do to get there, that effort now will pay off in the long run. You need a burning desire to improve what needs improving.

It's easy to say that you have this, but talk is cheap. We all know what it's like to have big plans but then watch them drift away without really knowing how or why it happened. Too often people miss out on the good things in life because they decide it's more comfortable where they are. That approach is not going to cut it here.

Meet Brendan and Danielle

So you want to know what's at stake? I'm going to introduce you to two business owners: Brendan and Danielle. They are fictional characters, but really they are like the business owners I meet every day. I've seen all this many, many times before.

Danielle's a nice woman with a young family. After ten years working for a major publisher she went out on her own and started a publishing business three years ago. She started off well, worked hard and had lots of clients. She didn't spend a lot of time working on building the business because she was always busy. She could always pay the bills on time so she thought her business was strong. Her accountant always smiled, and her customers always came back because she was good at what she did. Profit margins, cashflow, marketing, conversion rates and the like received little attention. She wasn't interested in 'that stuff'. She didn't know it, but her business had no underlying foundation.

Then the publishing industry changed, rapidly and unexpectedly. Book stores closed, people started turning to the internet for information, ebooks reduced profit margins. Before she knew it Danielle was behind on her bills, didn't have much work lined up and her accountant started looking a little worried.

Like many small business owners she thought the solution was simply to work harder. She stayed at the office longer and went in on weekends. She grabbed onto every opportunity she could, even if it wasn't very good for her business – very soon she was working crazy hours doing projects she didn't enjoy that put not much money in the bank. Once she got into the cycle of working hard each month to pay last month's overdue bills it became her normal way of operating because she didn't know how to get out of it. She became so focused on simply trying to stave off collapse that she didn't have the time or energy to make a change. Or at least that's what she thought.

It's been like this for Danielle for over a year now.

Does any of that sound familiar to you?

Now let's meet Brendan.

Brendan runs a small coffee shop in a little laneway in Melbourne and business is booming. Owning a coffee shop in Melbourne is tough – you don't have to walk far to find a quality coffee in Melbourne. But Brendan has built strong foundations for his business. He knows who his target market is and why his customers buy from him. He has a team of dedicated staff who are just as keen for the business to succeed as he is. He knows his finances inside out, always has enough cash to pay the bills, and has a clear direction and efficient systems. And because he has carefully created a business designed for long-term success he doesn't have to work ridiculous hours, doesn't get too stressed and always has money in his pocket. He never works weekends – that's what his great staff are for – and has plenty of time to pursue his passions away from work.

So what's the difference between Danielle and Brendan? Is Brendan smarter or harder working than Danielle? Is he better educated? Did he have more money behind him? Did he find the best location in Melbourne? Is he just lucky?

The answer to all of those questions is *no*. The only difference that matters between these two is that Brendan *made a decision to change*. That's right. You see, one year ago Brendan and Danielle were in exactly the same position…

When Brendan first opened his store three years ago he thought he had a great location. It was overlooking picturesque gardens on the edge of the CBD, and the afternoon sun flooded the courtyard. There was plenty of parking and it was close enough to the CBD shops that people could walk there. There was a McCafé on the same block but he thought that would attract different customers and wouldn't be a threat.

This great location was supposed to be the key to his success, but for the first two years there were more pigeons in his courtyard than customers and he had to repeatedly dive into his personal savings to stay afloat. He did some haphazard marketing and tried a few things on Facebook, but there was no real plan or direction. He was simply jumping at opportunities as they appeared without any real focus or strategy. He had concluded after about six months that his great location was actually not so awesome. He realised that when people came into the city they were usually in a hurry, and therefore would simply grab a coffee wherever it was convenient. They didn't want to sit in the sun and relax, they wanted to keep moving. There was always a queue at the McCafé.

But, rather than watch his dream disappear in a puff of coffee beans, he decided to fix things. He'd worked too hard to simply sit by and watch his dream die. After facing the stark reality that he had almost no personal cash left as a backup and another few months like this would put him out of business and into the poor house he decided it was time to make a change. He looked at himself in the mirror and confessed to having made a mess of things. He'd worked hard and had the best intentions, but he hadn't educated himself about business the way he needed to. He had placed too much faith in the location of his store, and when that turned out to be a problem he had no other skills or knowledge to help him. His coffee shop had become deadwood and it was up to him to turn it around.

After getting the help he needed to address his problems and build his business Brendan made the difficult but correct decision to move his store. Whatever he had thought about why people would buy from him, he had turned out to be wrong and it was time to face up to that. After lots of research into where might be a more appropriate location for him, he used the last remaining funds in the business to pay for the move. It was a risk but he knew he had to do it. It was move or close.

The new location was not picturesque but it was in a city lane that was used as a thoroughfare between two busy city streets. From day one at his new location the cash register was ringing all day. The strong start gave him the opportunity to hire more staff, and – again, rather than rushing in – he did his homework very carefully and hired the right people. He started setting monthly goals, studied his finances, learned about cashflow, tested and measured different products, created systems to streamline the business – all the things he failed to do at the beginning because he thought his location would do all the work for him.

And so, six months later...

Brendan's business has grown another 20% and he's thinking about taking over the empty store next door. He has his confidence back and is running things like the CEO of a major company. The business is humming. Brendan no longer makes coffee; he spends his time planning how to make things bigger and better, leaving the day-to-day things to his staff. And because he is no longer stressed and has more money and time, his life away from work is great as well.

It's taken a few unexpected turns, but his dreams for his business are now coming true.

And Danielle? She also has more time on her hands – because her business went under. She fought valiantly but she just couldn't bring herself to make the changes she needed to. She was sure things would turn around. What she was doing had worked in the past; she just had to wait for 'things to pick up again'. But they didn't. Danielle's industry left her behind and she didn't face up to it. Her resistance was stronger than her desire to change, and her vision for what her business could be simply wasn't strong enough. She took the all-too-common 'she'll be right' approach and ended up where this approach always does. Holding on and hoping has never been a recipe for success.

Now she works in a booming little coffee shop in a laneway in Melbourne.

 **CHAPTER GEMS**

- So where will you be in six months time? Will you be Brendan or will you be Danielle?

- Do you have the will and the desire to turn deadwood to diamonds or are you going to take the 'she'll be right' approach, with a few prayers and sacrifices to the gods thrown in for good measure?

- Being honest with yourself is the first step to finding clarity for your business.

- Finding clarity will set you on your journey to business success.

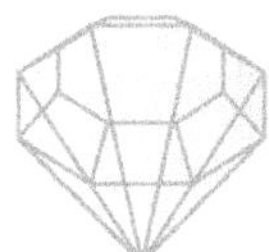

2. YOUR FORMULA FOR TRANSFORMATION

Turning your business around starts with turning yourself around. I have all sorts of great formulas, techniques and systems I will give you in this book, but if you haven't truly committed to making a change then they won't help you. It's as simple as that. I know for a fact they work when resistance is overcome, and I know for a fact they don't when resistance wins. There will be effort and sacrifice and perhaps some painful decisions along the way, but I promise you they won't be as painful as staying on the path to destruction.

THE FORMULA

There's a formula that will help you discover what it takes to make this leap, to recognise and acknowledge it's time to make a change. It's a formula that will help you truly confront your current situation and start making plans for how you are going to start transforming yourself and your business.

Here's the **Formula for Transformation:**

(Frustrations × Desired outcomes) + Clarity > Resistance to transform

I've been helping small businesses achieve big business success for many years, so I know what I'm talking about. And if you don't understand this formula and have it tipped in your favour your chances of turning deadwood into diamonds are slim.

So what does this formula mean?

THE FIVE KEY FRUSTRATIONS OF MOST SMALL BUSINESS OWNERS

Let's look at the left side of the above equation first. I'm quite certain you are feeling a sense of frustration and dissatisfaction with where you are right now in your business – and that's okay! Without that frustration you'd just sit around and watch and eat popcorn while your business evaporates. That frustration means *you don't want to sit idly by* while your business implodes and that's what will drive you to change.

In my many years working with small business I have found that there are generally five key frustrations that contribute to dissatisfaction with the business. I'd bet that they keep reappearing time and again. They are common problems that can send businesses to the wall. You may recognise some of them:

- cashflow problems
- being lonely and scared
- having a dysfunctional team
- being exhausted, stressed and having no time
- procrastination.

Let's look at each of these in turn.

1. Cashflow: People often run out of money before they run out of ideas. Cashflow is not just about how much you are earning, it is also about managing when that cash comes in and goes out, so that you always have dollars in the bank when bills are due.

2. Being lonely and scared. Running a small business can be daunting and lonely. Even if you manage a business with staff it's easy to feel isolated, alone and responsible for the success or failure of the company. Small business owners also often feel that they are burdening their families if they bring their stress home, further adding to the sense of isolation. Business owners often say to me, 'I can't keep going home every day and telling my partner about problems at work'.

3. Having a dysfunctional team. A dysfunctional team usually starts with the owner. If you haven't taken the proper care or don't know how to hire the right staff you are in trouble from day one. The right people will power you to success; the wrong people will put the brakes on your business.

4. Being exhausted, stressed and having no time. People often go into business for themselves because they think it will enhance their lifestyle and improve their work/life harmony, and it certainly will – if you get it right. But if your business hits problems it will have the exact opposite effect

– I've lost count of the number of small business owners I meet who say, 'I didn't think it would be like this – I'm still at the office at 9 o'clock at night and I go in on weekends. How did this happen?' That's often the point at which they come to me. People's first response to trouble is usually simply to work harder, rather than stopping and having a good hard look at what is causing the problems. Not only is being tired and stressed not a lot of fun, it also leads to poor decision-making, which only adds to the problems.

5. **Procrastination.** This is the biggest single issue to overcome – no matter what else you have figured out about your business: if you don't get off your backside and start to make changes things are only going to get worse. I guarantee it. The inability to make a decision can be caused by paralysis by analysis. Or maybe you don't know what you don't know. Or maybe it's the fear. Whatever it is holding you back, you must identify and overcome it.

THE FIVE KEY DESIRED OUTCOMES FOR MOST SMALL BUSINESS OWNERS

What about your desired outcomes? This is your view of how you want things to look when you come out the other side. It's often the inverse of your current situation; if one of your frustrations is you don't have enough time on your hands, the desired outcome would be to have more free time. If one of your frustrations is not having enough money in the bank, your desired outcome would be to have enough cash to live comfortably. Your frustrations are what you are trying to leave behind – your desired outcomes are what you are aiming for.

Here are the five key desired outcomes I come across most often:

◆ clarity and confidence
◆ more clients in our desired target market
◆ profit growth
◆ having a champion team
◆ more time to spend with my loved ones.

Let's have a look at each of these in turn:

1. Clarity and confidence. Clarity breeds confidence. The more clarity you have the more confidence you will have to move forward. Confidence by itself is not enough. If you have confidence but are on the wrong track you are going nowhere very quickly. Most small business owners start their enterprise because they are particularly skilled at something and they are confident they can make a go of it on their own. But this confidence is often shaken with the realisation that starting a business versus growing a business are two very different things, and ultimately the business hits trouble. Restoring this confidence in themselves and their business is vital for success. They need clarity and they need to know that what they are doing is going somewhere.

2. More clients in our desired target market. The key here is *desired target market*. Getting new clients is often quite easy – just dropping your prices will do it. But that's not the road to sustainability. If it were *really* that easy your business would be booming right now. You need the *right* clients that you can build your business around.

3. Profit growth. An obvious desire, but how do you get there? It's also not just about profit in the pocket but profit in the heart. It's about leading a more fulfilling life and feeling you are making a difference to those around you. It's about being able to take your family on that holiday you promised or being able to buy your kids those new runners.

4. Having a champion team. The right staff will be a massive boost to your business. You are not great at everything, so plug the gaps in your skill set with people who do those things better than you do. You also need people better at what you do than you are. This is the ultimate result for your business so you can move on to bigger and better things. If you have a great centre half forward you don't need to worry about that position any more. At the start you might have to train them but later when you are bigger you can hire the best because they will want to work for you. You don't want a business full of people who hide in the lunch room because they don't know what they are doing or who count the minutes to the weekend from 9 am on Monday.

5. I want more time to spend with my loved ones. This is the holy grail for every small business owner I meet. Every one of them. While they are proud of their businesses and love what they do, having a successful and sustainable business is a means to an end, and the end is actually being able to spend less time in the business and more time doing the things in life that truly matter. Personally I have a rule that I never work on weekends. *Never.* Wouldn't you love to be able to do that?

How would it be if you could achieve all of those goals?

Does it seem impossible? Does it look like something other people can do but not you? Well, it's not. Believe me – this is what I do. I see small business owners reach these goals every day, and often more quickly than they expected to. And it's not because they are geniuses, have millions of dollars behind them or have invented the next Facebook; it's because they looked at their businesses and decided it was time to change, they got the help they needed, and they committed to the process. And there's no reason why you can't do this too. Right?

So, back to our formula…

CLARITY

What are you going to do to get going? What are you going to do to escape this hole you are currently in? How are you going to move forward? The moment you have clarity about what is possible and about your desired outcomes is the moment you can get going. At this stage you don't need to know all the steps along the way, but you do need to have enough belief and enough traction to start. Just recognising what your business could be if it was bigger and stronger can be the first step. You may not have all the answers right now and that's fine; you will by the end of this book.

RESISTANCE TO TRANSFORM

Now, on the right-hand side of the equation we have resistance to transform. I'd like to be able to say this in a deep, menacing voice, like something out of a horror movie, because it seems to have that effect on people. But because this is a book and not a movie you'll just have to use your imagination.

The resistance to transform has stood in the way of many a dream. It freezes people on the spot for no good reason; it causes them to look backwards rather than forward; it leads them to make poor decisions even when the correct way ahead seems obvious.

Why does this happen? Why do they become stuck? Why is it okay to stay with the status quo? Why is it acceptable not to create a better outcome?

Sometimes people are used to being frustrated and feeling inadequate. When a business starts to go backwards rather than forward confidence takes a hit and this leads to resistance. It's an understandable feeling, but one that can be overcome.

The people you grew up with and have around you also affect your ability to take charge. Maybe when you were growing up people said you weren't good enough or didn't encourage you. Maybe you have people around you now who are telling you it's too hard or too risky and you should just get out. Having these negative influences can be a real drain on your energy and commitment.

Fear also leads to resistance – fear of failure and fear of success. Fear of failure is easy to understand: I could lose lots of money or my house, I'll let people down, I'll feel like a failure. But fear of success can also be a problem. If you don't have a clear plan, or confidence in where you are going, the thought of being successful can be quite daunting. Will I be able to handle the business if it gets larger? Do I have the skills to manage more staff or make bigger deals? Will I be comfortable managing larger amounts of money or opening a new store?

So, how will *you* go with this formula?

EXERCISE: The moment of truth

The moment of Brutal Truth comes when you sit down with a blank piece of paper and decide to complete this exercise for yourself. This is a very important step, so do it properly. Don't just scribble a few things down in your 12-minute lunch break.

1. Get up early one morning before everybody else, and before you've even made a coffee or read the paper, go into a quiet room and sit and think about it.

2. Draw a line down the middle of your page, and on the left-hand side write the heading 'frustrations'. Then, think about what's troubling you, the real issues that are holding your business back. You know very well what they are; you live with them every day. Don't think about how you're going to solve these problems for now, just write them down. Chances are you will have a few of the ones that we discussed earlier.

    Frustrations:

    ____

    ____

    ____

3. Then, in the right-hand column write down your desired outcomes. Be realistic but dream big as well. Don't be afraid. What does your ideal business look like? What does your ideal life look like? What would make you excited to get out of bed in the morning, like when you first started your business? What does it look like if you're not stressed all the time or worried about where your next client is going to come from?

    Desired outcomes:

    ____

    ____

    ____

    Here's the key to this formula: you need to be brutally honest about your frustrations and what the desired outcomes could be. Dare to dream. Be bold. What would your ultimate business and life look like?

My ultimate business will look like this:

____

____

____

What could be the first steps in moving away from my frustrations towards desired outcomes?

Do I have the passion required to move towards my vision or move away from my pain?

4. Now, what does clarity mean to you? Are you absolutely 100% clear about your business goals? Do you know exactly what you do and why you do it? Do you know with clarity who your customers are, how to reach them and why they buy from you? Being clear about every aspect of your business is vital if you are going to move forward. Write down now what clarity means to you – succinctly summarise what your business does, who your customers are and why they buy from you. (This is just the start of clarity – we'll go into it in much more depth throughout the book and your answers to these questions will most likely change as you read and learn. If you don't have clarity about your business yet, that's fine! That's what I'm here for – just do your best for now, and keep reading.)

Clarity:

____

____

____

5. Now, here's a moment of Brutal Truth. Have a look at your business and your life, and find out what is holding you back. What obstacles are you putting in your own way that stop you reaching your goals? The fact that you are reading this book means you are aware of resistance in your business. What is it? I know you know. Write it down here...

Resistance to transform:

____

____

____

6. Are your desired outcomes and is your frustration with where you are strong enough to overcome your resistance? Is your desire for change and improvement and a better life stronger than your worries and fears? Is your vision big enough and strong enough to overcome the roadblocks you will face? This is a defining line that requires your honest assessment of where you are and where you want to go. This is a massive driver for you to get going. Once you recognise that your desired outcomes are greater than your resistance you can take the first steps. If they are not, you won't go anywhere. You won't have the required determination. If you are convinced you are deadwood that's all you ever will be.

    Don't be alarmed if you had trouble answering any of these questions, or if you still have resistance. Most people don't even give themselves permission to write this down and so they won't understand that it's even possible, so be proud of making this first step. The moment you move forward with creating a list of what you are dissatisfied with, and what it could look like if it was bigger and better, and then dare to put your desired outcomes on the other side, is a major break through.

    Even if you still have frustrations, you've moved forward just by doing this exercise, so well done!

Right now you may be thinking, 'But I don't *know* how to make the changes my business needs…' And that's okay! That's my job! That's exactly why I'm here. In this book we're going to look at all of the issues above and much more. I have all the advice, strategies, systems, tips and formulas you need. I make this promise to you: **this book will bring great benefits to you and your business if you make the**

commitment and follow through. But the one thing I *cannot* do for you is make you have this epiphany. That's… entirely…up…to…you.

 ## CHAPTER GEMS

- Identifying your frustrations will start to bring clarity.
- Then you can shape your desired outcomes for your business.
- Overcome your fears that are holding you back.
- Face your demons – the moment of truth has arrived.

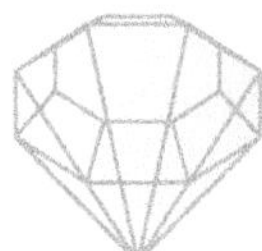

3. THE #1 BIG OUTCOME

What is *your* number one commitment to your clients? What is their **point A** and **point B**, and what is the **bridge you build** to get them across? What is the core of your business?

I refer to this as the **#1 Big Outcome** and it requires two or three layers of strategic thinking. It's not as simple as saying, 'People come to me when they want furniture'. You have to think about *why they want the furniture*. This can be one of the most difficult things to do and only a small number of people get to this level of thinking about their business. Sometimes it takes lots of reflection, sometimes it happens by osmosis – they just figure it out. Once you've dug deeper into your customers' needs and frustrations and become clear on why people buy from you, you are in the perfect place to create the ideal proposition for them. You are emotionally connecting. You know the bridge you can build and you understand why they want to cross it. This helps give you short-term survival but also long-term focus and understanding.

WHAT BRIDGE DO YOU BUILD?

People spend money because they have a problem they want solved. Essential to the growth of your business is having clarity about exactly what this problem is and how you are going to take your clients from their current state of frustration to freedom.

Many small businesses have become deadwood because the owners didn't understand exactly what their clients wanted from them. If you don't understand this everything else you do will be built on shaky foundations. Every successful business provides a bridge for their customers to get them from A to B. Have a think about it now before you read on. **What do you do for your customers? Why do they come to you?** Write your answer down now – we'll be coming back to it later.

Consider the following businesses.

* What does a plumber sell? A plumber sells and installs pipes, taps, washers and hoses. Right? Wrong.
* What does a hairdresser sell? Hair-cuts? Nope.
* What service does a mechanic provide? Fixing cars? Not even close.

Let's have a closer look and see what these businesses are *really* selling to their clients.

Most of us have experienced a plumbing emergency. It's frustrating – but have a think about *why* it's frustrating. If you're getting ready for work and your hot water system blows up you don't think to yourself, 'Hey, I better call the plumber. He has lots of great pipes, taps, washers and hoses and clearly I need some new ones. I can't wait to see what he's got.' You think, 'Bugger, now I'm going to be late for work.' Most people have not the slightest interest in how or why their plumbing works, they just care that it does. So a plumber is not selling pipes, taps, washers and hoses, he's selling comfort and convenience. He's selling hot showers. He's selling getting to work on time. He's selling not having to worry about that stuff because he can do it. It's not actually about the products at all.

Why do we get a hair-cut? To be more aerodynamic? No. Because we feel better and more confident when we look good, and this flows into every aspect of our lives. Hairdressers sell self-esteem.

And the mechanic? Again, it's not about the widgets and doodads, it's about what the car means in the customer's life. For most people car troubles are very disruptive. The car gets you to work, you can visit your friends, it saves time, it brings you home right to your door. You can get the kids safely from here to there. Fixing customers' cars is putting the convenience back into their life.

As you get clear on the needs of your customers you can begin to understand what they really want from you and you can profitably deliver to your target audience.

EXERCISE: Answering the 7 Whys

If you're not sure what your #1 Big Outcome is, you can try a little exercise known as the **7 Whys**. It's not hard. Start by asking, 'Why do people come to me?' If, for example, you are selling furniture, your obvious answer is, 'They need new furniture'. But that's only the first **why**. You need to go deeper...

Why do people come to me?
They need new furniture.

Why do they need new furniture?
Because their old furniture is worn out.

Why does this matter?
Because they want their house to look nice.

Why does this matter?
Because this makes them feel good.

Why does it make them feel good?
Because it makes them feel successful.

Why does this matter?
Because this builds their self-esteem and makes them feel confident.

Why does this matter?
Because when people feel confident they are happier and can live a better life.

Count them – that's seven whys. Seven steps to get to the *real reason* people buy new furniture.

For me, in my business, the obvious answer might be something like, 'People come to me to make their business more profitable'. And that's true. But it's not the deeper, underlying, true motivation of why they come to me. They know that if their business performs better they will have more money and more free time to do the things in life they really want to do *away from their business*. So it's not actually about the business at all. It's about quality of life. I know this about my business and my clients and it's incorporated into everything we do. Everything. It's non-negotiable. Everything!

When you dig down deep enough and find the answer for your business this becomes a source of culture and purpose for you and your staff. It becomes an anchor and a point of alignment with your clients. It's what your business will become known for. It's not about marketing or creating a tag line; it's about having clarity and truly understanding what you offer. It becomes a measuring stick for your business. It's the #1 Big Outcome.

It will provide fire in your belly because you will see how you can help people and improve their lives. This is important because if you are only motivated by money, one day that motivation will run out when you reach a certain amount of dollars in the bank. But if you are achieving and helping your customers you are going to feel good and feel aligned with what you are doing.

Remember when I asked you earlier to think about why your customers come to you? Do you want to try again now? Remember, it's *not* about the widgets and doodads you sell. It's about why they will emotionally connect with you. Use the seven whys and see how far you can get. I do this exercise with my clients all the time and many of them get stumped after three or four whys. They start going in circles or simply run out of answers. Keep going until you get to what you believe is at the heart of the matter. What do they *really* want from you? How can you take them from frustration to freedom? How can you provide them with a better quality of life? If you haven't done this before it can be a real breakthrough for you and your business. It will give you greater confidence to serve your clients like there's no tomorrow. Think of it like an Olympic athlete: what sport are you in? What's your best event? Where will you win gold?

What's *your* #1 Big Outcome?

 **CHAPTER GEMS**

- Identifying your #1 Big Outcome will give you clarity in your business.

- Your customers will help you identify this.

- Answer the seven whys to give you further clarity.

4. INVESTMENT VS RETURN ON INVESTMENT

Having clarity within your business is one thing, but are you clear about what your customers want? After all, it is your customers who will make or break your business.

Sometimes small business owners get a little tongue-tied and challenged when it comes to talking to future clients about what their investment will be and what return they will get. Especially when starting out, some entrepreneurs find it difficult to talk about 'the money side of things'. This is especially difficult if you don't know what your #1 Big Outcome is.

Investment vs return on investment (ROI) for your customers is about clarity, and the more confident you are about how you get clients from A to B the more clearly you'll be able to convey this to your clients. Why should people use you and not your competitors?

THE FOUR Fs

There are all sorts of reasons people make a purchase. What are you *really* selling to your customers? You need to spend time to figure this out. There are four main types of returns you can provide. These are very important for you to remember and strategise to achieve for your clients. I call these the **Four Fs:**

- Financial ROI
- Feelings ROI
- Physical ROI – okay, I know it's not an 'F' but it sounds like it!
- Fire in the belly ROI.

Financial ROI

This one is obvious. If a client invests $100, $1,000 or $10,000 with you, what return will they get on this? You should be able to answer this easily and accurately – if you can't you don't have enough clarity about what you do. If you can't establish a percentage return, what is your rule of thumb? As a rule of thumb, I aim to provide a minimum of ×10 return for all my clients.

Feelings ROI

The business owner has told the family that when things pick up they are going to Disneyland! What can you do for your client to help with this? This is going beyond just the financial return on investment. It's the feel-good factor. It's about being emotionally charged. A great example is Apple computers; it's not just about the machine, it's about the feeling you get owning and using one.

Physical ROI

A hair-cut is not going to give you a financial return unless you are a movie star or a model, but you get an emotional return on investment because it makes you look and feel good. I'm sure you know somebody who spends a *lot* of money on hair-cuts. Can you make people look 10 years younger? Or can you give them a change of environment? Or change their surroundings or space?

Fire in the belly ROI

This is the most critical return you can give somebody – it's putting a fire in their belly. This fire is what my clients are often seeking, even though they might not know this. The biggest drag on most deadwood businesses is not a lack of knowledge or resources but a lack of direction and determination. Once the fire is lit they are off, but they need somebody else to light the fire. What they are buying from me is purpose. Is this something you can do? The moment you seriously connect and it fuels the rage to just get going, that's massive. When you can do that for your client it's game on. What about gym memberships? It's not just about the equipment, it's about the motivation provided by being a member and hanging out with other like-minded people.

The most obvious return on investment, no matter what you do, is a financial one. The financial return comes from how much money people spend buying from you. Most people will shop around when making a purchase, and a key thing they are considering is price. They want to know how much they have to spend if they buy from you and what they will get for their money. If your product costs $500 more than your nearest competitor, what are they getting for this extra outlay?

There are businesses that obviously lend themselves to a financial ROI, but you can't stop there. It's your responsibility to understand and cover all of the different types of ROI. This may be difficult but you must push through. You must get to an answer. Think outside the square.

Let's look at my business as an example; although I can easily point to the financial return people will achieve when they come to me, I know this isn't the *real* reason they come, *even if they don't know this themselves*. They want their businesses to perform better so they have money and time to do other things, so they are after a *feelings* return, not just a financial one. The extra money they earn will also allow them to improve their *physical* environment, such as affording to buy a new car or moving to a better office, and the clarity and focus they gain from starting to make changes to their business will provide the *fire in the belly*.

A *feelings* ROI can be giving people the confidence to try something new by teaching them a new skill, a *physical* ROI can be selling things that help people organise their homes or their work. It's your responsibility to figure out what it is they are going to get as a return on investment. They may be after something they can't articulate or they are not even consciously aware of – you must be able to discover what that is. There are potential clients out there who are yet to come into your circle of influence – why will they come to you? You need to be able to have an open and honest conversation about what it will cost them and what they will receive from you in what timeframe.

TALK TO YOUR CUSTOMERS

If you're having trouble finding clarity around this, you have a great resource at your disposal: your existing clients! Speak to people you have already served. Ask them why they came to you in the first place and ask them what needs you met for them. Did they get what they expected from you? Was there anything missing? While you're at it, get some on-the-record testimonials from your most delighted clients. This will provide what is known as tribal proof (or social proof) for your business. (Taking credit is something we all need to get better at. Delighted customers become advocates and raving fans. They have tested your business and said, 'Yes it's real. It's authentic. It is amazing.' Take time to celebrate with your clients. Get the taste of success – this will help motivate you for the next level of success.)

Here are a few things you can do to help your business communicate with, and get valuable feedback from, your clients:

1. You have to show up when needed, not just when you're paid to do so. Sometimes you have to go a little bit above and beyond for your customers.

2. You have to be committed. It has to be part of your DNA to get constant feedback. You can't just surprise them out of the blue and ask them what they think.

3. You must monitor your progress in relation to your scoreboard. It's great to get feedback but you need a reference point. You need to be able to see progress.

4. Get 360-degree feedback. Sometimes you need to hire third-party specialists to get feedback on your behalf.

Clients will also want to know what the potential risks are when they invest with you; that is, what could potentially go wrong when dealing with your business? It's okay not to be bullet-proof and it's okay to be challenged. It's okay for 93% of your clients to achieve the desired result. In fact, that's a great success rate! It's how you deal with something when it goes wrong that defines your business. If you think you are achieving 100% somebody will beat you because that means you are staying still.

Your clients also need to pull their weight. In most cases it's the human element that lets you down. For example, for me to achieve success with my clients they need to put in the effort and take ownership for what we discuss and agree that we will do – if they don't do that there's nothing I can do to help. 'Going to' isn't going to cut it. You need people who just 'do'. That's your target market. When you are clear about your product and what it does, you can find the target audience that's going to bring it home and nail it.

You can wait for growth but you can't wait for opportunities – you have to reach out and grab them. There are potential clients out there who are ready to invest their time and money – it's your job to make sure they do it with you. Are you giving your clients the return on investment they are after? This is the value proposition for your business. Once you have confirmed the size of your target market you must go to it not wait for it. With the number of options available to people these days, now more than ever it's a *go to* market not a *wait for* market. The moment you own this and wear it like a glove it's game on and you are winning.

HOURLY RATE IDENTITY CRISIS

Have you thought about the investment you are putting in to your business? Are you working for nothing? Or are you satisfied with the return on your personal exertion investment?

I find that about 75% of small business owners have a disconnect here. The issue of maximising the return on each hour you work can be a tricky one and it can be another thing that is holding you back. I call this the **Hourly Rate Identity Crisis.**

To see whether you've hit this crisis, answer the questions below:

1. How much do you charge out for your time an hour?

   ____

2. How many hours on average do you work a week?

   ____

3. How much did you pay yourself last month?

   ____

4. Is there a disconnect?

   ____

Chances are you have worked out what an hour of your time is worth, based on your skills and experience and the industry you are in. This isn't where the problem usually lies. The issue is, *how many hours a week do you actually earn that rate?*

Time is a finite resource so it's crucial that you put it to good use. If you have an identity crisis here it can spell trouble.

What activities should you be doing to give your business the best outcomes for each hour you work? Be clear about who you are, what you do, and why. Think about your #1 Big Outcome. The best opportunity for your business is to build one reputation for doing one thing, then add to it. Ask yourself, what's my one thing? What am I actually worth an hour? Why? What are the activities that I do daily, weekly and monthly that help me ensure I achieve that rate?

The next question is, how many hours a week do you work on average? Most business people I know can answer this question quite easily, so now you should have two figures: an hourly rate that you believe you are worth and the average number of hours you work per week.

Now you can calculate the following equation:

What you are worth per hour × How many hours you work on average per week

Consider the answer carefully.

Now, here's the kicker: *when was the last time you took home a weekly pay cheque close to that amount?* Sadly, for some business owners the answer is *never*. If this is you, this is a *huge wasted opportunity for your business.*

So if you're not taking home close to that amount each week, or even some weeks, or even occasionally, what's the problem? If you're not skiving off and going to the beach then clearly you're spending time at the office doing tasks you shouldn't be doing. Yes that's right, you *shouldn't be doing!* I'm not saying those tasks don't need to be done, just that they don't need to be done *by you.*

What about if you *are* achieving this every week? Does that mean everything is peachy? Not at all. If you are reaching this target every week your hourly rate is too low! Nobody can work at their maximum achievable hourly rate every single hour for a whole week, let alone week after week, so if you *think* you are doing this you need to increase your hourly rate. There is clearly room for you to do so and you are currently missing out on this opportunity.

 ## CHAPTER GEMS

- Identifying the different returns on investment will bring clarity to your business.

- Feedback is a wonderful thing.

- Are you getting a fair return on your own daily exertion?

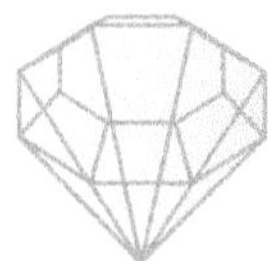

5. FOCUSING ON YOUR STRENGTHS

Once you start asking some Brutal Truth questions and facing up to reality you will realise that a lot of time you spend in your business is wasted opportunity. Too many small business owners spend time on things that earn a low hourly rate for their skill set. It's a very common problem. Many entrepreneurs start out alone with little cash, and so they get into the habit of doing everything themselves and trying to cut costs while they do so. This can be okay – and is often necessary – in the very early days of getting the business off the ground but, once you are past that stage, having a Lone Ranger complex will be a massive hindrance to the growth of your business.

DELEGATION IS A WONDERFUL THING

Have a look at what you are doing each day. For each activity you do that is not at your maximum hourly rate, you have four options. I like to make things easy for my clients to remember, so I call these the **DOTS Options**[*]:

- **Delegating:** I'll come back to this point often: you need a great team around you. Not good, great. And what's the point of a great team if you don't delegate to them?

- **Outsourcing:** You can outsource just about anything these days without too much expense and you can trust that the job will be done right. Some small business owners see this as a cost they can't afford, but your maximum hourly rate will be more than the hourly rate you pay for outsourcing (and if it's not, perhaps you need to start an outsourcing business instead!), so you come out in front and you can be spending your time more productively.

- **Terminating:** Sometimes you'll find that a task can simply be done away with altogether. Plenty of businesses have old habits and systems that they could get rid of but nobody has stopped to look at them closely. Or maybe there's something you do five times a week that really only needs your attention twice a week.

- **Systematising/Automating:** Can you set up processes that reduce or eliminate time spent on a task? For example, can you set up your website so that orders go direct to your suppliers and you don't have to send products out?

Delegating and outsourcing are essential to the growth of your business but these are two areas people often struggle with. Let's have a look at some common challenges to outsourcing and delegating.

---

[*] From *The 4-Hour Workweek* concept, by Timothy Ferriss.

I don't know what I don't know

Sometimes we just become so caught up in the day-to-day craziness that we don't even stop to consider other options. Make the time to stop, look and listen; find out what the issues are in your business and how you can address them. You can't solve a problem that you don't know about.

Trust

This is common problem for entrepreneurs. They are so used to being experts in their field and doing everything themselves that they are reluctant to hand responsibility to others. If you want something done properly you have to do it yourself, right? Wrong! The tasks for which you earn your highest hourly rate are best done by you, but let me tell you something: for most other tasks in your business there are people out there who are better at it than you – and that's fantastic! Chances are you are not an expert bookkeeper, or warehouse manager, or marketing manager, or customer liaison, but too many small business owners try to wear too many hats and don't perform any of these tasks as well as they could be done. You need to trust your staff and service-providers. You don't need to be afraid of outsourcing to Bangladesh or maybe even Russia.

Too busy

As a business coach this response drives me nuts! The reason you think you are too busy today is that you didn't stop and make changes yesterday. You must make the time to improve things today; that's the only way you'll be less busy tomorrow. Got it?

Putting things in a format people can follow

Because small business owners get used to doing everything

themselves they often develop their own unique methods and this becomes an impediment to delegation. But this is an easy problem to overcome – you just need to spend some time developing processes that you can easily pass on. It may take a bit of extra effort now but I guarantee it will save you time in the long run.

We can't afford it

Let me dismiss this one for you here and now – if you want to grow your business you can't afford *not* to delegate and outsource. Even if you are outstanding at what you do, if you don't let go of managing the day-to-day issues in your business you are putting a ceiling on how much you can grow, and that ceiling is how many hours you can work in a week. If you think you can't afford it, can you afford not to? If you are this close to the edge something has to change.

If any of these are holding you back you have to address them – now. You need clarity about where your best work is done and what is getting in the way of growth. It might be you. The sooner you do this, the faster you will build a business that gives you the outcomes you deserve.

HOW TO BEST SPEND YOUR TIME?

To work out what you should be doing with your time just figure out the three to five activities that are your strengths.

My key strengths are:

1. ____

2. ____

3. ____

4. ____

5. ____

It can't be more than this or you'll just start getting bogged down again. Most of my clients have about five activities that they are really good at within their skill set and are their highest hourly rate activities. For most small business owners these activities will be related to the skills that got them into the business in the first place. If you're a graphic designer you didn't go into business to spend time doing the accounts, chasing new clients or firefighting problems as they arise. There are other people who will be better at these things than you so let them do it; then you can spend your time doing what *you* do best.

Even if you are on your own you can still find somebody to help keep you accountable. I've been getting coached for 22 years. I still get coached today. I still write a cheque for somebody to help me improve my business. Once you've identified these activities, answer this question: how much of your time each week as a percentage is invested in these specific tasks? The difference between how much time you *could* be spending on these tasks and how much you *are* spending on these tasks is your gap to creating a business that at some point will give you freedom of time and freedom of money.

Your long-term goal is to spend 80% of your time on your highest-rate activities, the good-old 80/20 rule. No matter how well you do you won't get to 100%. As the leader and key decision-maker in your business you will always be required to spend some time on more mundane decisions and tasks. Problems always crop up and we all need to take a break during the day. The most successful business people I know are at 80% and that's great.

Even if you are on your own this is achievable. There are

all sorts of excellent outsourcing services that cater to small businesses. Trust yourself to find the right people and guide them well, and then trust them to do the job for you. Give them good systems, wind them up and let them go. The world has become a smaller village and the days of dodgy overseas outsourcing are long gone.

Once you start to address these harsh truths about how you're spending your time and you start walking the walk you will quickly learn that you shouldn't be making the coffee, going to the post office and chasing unpaid bills. It's about having a strategic mindset. How will your next hour best be used to grow your business? You have to hold yourself accountable, and this can be tough because it can mean facing the fact that you haven't been working as well as you could have been. I see it all the time: people think the solution to a struggling business is to work harder, but it's not. It's to work *better*.

YOUR ALTERNATIVE DIARY SYSTEM

A proactive step you can take to help you get on top of your hours is to start a new diary system, which I call your **Default Diary**. At the start of each week, plot out each day so that 50% of your time is spent on doing the tasks you've identified as being the best use of your time. It's up to you exactly how you do this: 60 or 90 minute blocks of time can be good. Then you can block in other time for lower hourly rate tasks and for the inevitable unexpected things that pop up during your work week. Do this carefully and make sure you are at 50/50, and then put this schedule in your diary for the next four weeks. This will give you 50% structured time that is uninterrupted and highly productive at your highest hourly rate, and then 50% unstructured time for when you are getting slammed from pillar to post – we all know this happens in business no matter what plans you put in place.

Why not aim for 80% straight away? Because this will be a significant change to the way you work, and aiming for 80% right off the bat will be tough. Rather than helping, you might become frustrated that you didn't get there and throw the whole idea away because it didn't work. So start with 50% over four weeks and do whatever is needed to make this happen. It's a crucial step towards turning your business into a diamond.

It can be harder than you think to make this happen, so be happy with your progress as long as you keep heading in the right direction. If you reach 25% over four weeks this is a good step forward because most small business owners don't even operate at this level. Over time you can work your way to 80%, which is where the best of the best hang out. Once you get to this level you will stop calling it your Default Diary and it will just become your diary, because once you've seen how it works, why would you go back? Make this part of the DNA of your business.

THE RUBBER HITS THE ROAD

A lack of focus and discipline allows bad habits to kick in. However, you must stay true here. You must push through. The rubber hits the road when you create the discipline of time management. Inefficiency is a key leak in many businesses. If you can get through this you are half way there. Changing the diary is a point where I often see people run into trouble. It's a tangible step that requires making changes to what they do every day. It's not easy. I'll be the first person to tell you that. If it were easy you'd be making a million dollars a year right now. This is where a lack of confidence, a lack of trust in others and fear of failure (or success) can start to kick in. You have to find out why you are getting in the way of your own success and then rectify the situation. What is the Brutal Truth in your business?

All businesses face obstacles as they grow. Some will deal with them efficiently and with confidence, others will let them linger and just hope things get better by themselves. Are you going to get on the dance floor and do your dance or are you going to keep standing with your back to the wall and watch while others have all the fun?

Success in business is all about getting **brilliant at the basics**. Not good, brilliant. You don't need to be the smartest guy in the room, or the most wealthy, or to have the biggest company. You do need the honesty to look at your business and make a truthful assessment of where you are, and then you need the determination to do something about it. And then you need to get brilliant at the basics.

 ## CHAPTER GEMS

- Identify your strengths and learn to delegate anything that is not maximising your return on your time.
- Your long-term goal is to spend 80% of your time on your highest-rate activities.
- The alternative diary system will help you.

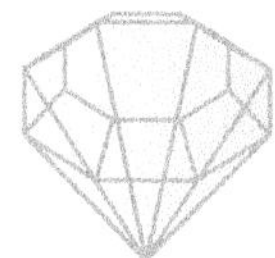

6. SMALL STEPS TO GREAT IMPROVEMENT

THE HOUR OF POWER

No, it's not an hour of inspirational television. The **Hour of Power** is about putting aside just one hour a week to think big – REALLY, REALLY BIG.

Once you've embraced the clarity of how to spend your time more profitably, what would it look like if you invest just one hour per week with an added zero on your hourly rate? If you're worth $100 an hour, what sort of work could you be doing that generates $1,000 an hour? What high-value strategic work could you be doing once a week for which you are going to hit it out of the ball park? What long-term planning could you do that will give you a 10× return? What new product or service can you come up with? What new market can you identify? In this one hour you can knock on that big door you never thought would open, you can call that big client you were always scared of, you can tackle that competitor who is currently ten times your size. It's about daring to dream. For just one hour throw away all those restrictions you've placed on yourself and just go for it. This is another disturbance in your business. Think BIG.

If you can't think big and dream big then you'll never be big. It's a barometer for your future success. So, in this one hour, don't just think about growing your business, think about its true potential, what it could be if you broke all the chains holding you back right now. Whatever you aim for is the best you will achieve, so if you think you can only grow by 10% in the next year that's the best you can hope for because you'll make all of your decisions based on this assumption. But what would happen if you went for 100% growth in the next year? Impossible? Certainly not. I've seen it happen many times. A key ingredient has *always* been thinking big and believing it can be done.

Don't think you have that extra hour to spare? What about the time you've freed up in your diary by delegating, out-sourcing, terminating and systemising! Now you're putting your time to much better use. Mark it in your diary. Now. The Hour of Power.

When you start to see the results of thinking big you'll want to find two of those hours. And then three. That's when the miracle occurs. That's when the light-bulb goes on and you can see that maybe you're not deadwood after all and that you can turn things around. Now you are working at a higher level. This is how you turn an everyday business into a profit machine.

CAN YOU IMPROVE BY 220% IN ONE YEAR?

That may sound like a lot, but I'm going to answer this question for you: you can – by improving just 1% every day! That's right, there are about 220 working days a year, so if you commit yourself to getting just 1% better *every single day that you are at work*, you'll be 220% better at your job in 12 months than you are now. How does that sound? I call this approach **Target 220**. It requires a deep desire to get better every day. You don't have to get 50% better by next week or 78% better by the end of the month. That's just not going to happen. But 1% better tomorrow? And then again the day after that? And again, and again? That is something you can achieve.

It's about aiming to be your **Personal Best**. If you don't have something driving you to be your Personal Best then chances are each day, each week and each month you are going to spend more time in mediocrity. But if you are clear about your opportunities, your strategic planning, and your use of time and money you can make the decision that you can be your Personal Best. You will be able to make 1% improvements each day. You can revolutionise and transform your business and yourself if you have the attitude of doing whatever it takes.

If you think that 1% isn't much, ask a scientist how important 0.0001% is. Ask a pilot how important one kilometre an hour is. Ask an Olympic athlete what 0.001 of a second means. Tiny increments are the difference between success and failure. If you want to be at the top of your industry at some point, ongoing 1% improvements will get you there.

If your aim is just to beat the other guy or to reach a certain level of profit, where do you go once you've done that? What is left to drive you and your business? The best coaches in sport will tell you they don't focus on winning games, they focus on the process. If they concentrate on getting better and doing the little things during games the wins will come. That's the attitude you need. If you just care about the win you've put a ceiling on your growth, but there are no limits when you are constantly aiming to be the best you can be.

Are you just flirting with success or are you going to chase it with all you've got? *Somebody* is going to win this race. Is it going to be you?

EXERCISE: 1% improvement

Write down five different ways you can improve by 1% each day in the next five days. Tick off each item each day as you complete it.

1. ____

2. ____

3. ____

4. ____

5. ____

How do you plan to maintain this mindset? If you've seen this work over five days, why would you let it go?

ARE YOU CLEAR YET?

Clarity is not about dollars and cents and it's not about how many clients you have. It's not about your marketing or your cashflow or your balance sheet or what new products you have coming next month. All this stuff comes later.

Clarity is about the DNA of your business. It's about what drives you and the people around you. It's the heart and soul of why you go into the office every day and the promise you make to your customers. It's an unshakeable confidence about who you are and why you do what you do. The better and deeper the sense of clarity, the higher the level of confidence, and this provides the relentless drive for you and your business to be the best they can be. What makes it happen is the business leader saying *I will*. But if you don't have confidence, trust and self-discipline you can't expect others to.

I can give you 95% of what you need, but the mindset of being your Personal Best is up to you. There's no such thing as 99% compliance. You're enrolled or you're not, you're serving a purpose or you're not, you're maximising your opportunities or you're not. You're at your Personal Best or you're not. It's an ethos and it's a culture for you and your business.

Don't drop your bundle to do this stuff – you can't profit if you are letting down the people you are already serving – but *make sure it gets done*. Don't think you are going to reach the promised land tomorrow but know that you will reach it with confidence, discipline and execution. It will be a bit harder before it gets easier, but when you're polishing your diamond rather than staring at deadwood you will know it was all worth it.

When you have clarity, confidence follows.

 ## CHAPTER GEMS

- Allocate an hour a week to allow yourself to think big.

- Dare to dream bigger.

- Set yourself small 1% improvement targets.

- Adopt the identity of a 1%-improvement-every-day-individual.

- Drive yourself to achieve your personal best.

CASE STUDY: The Drain Man (Aust) Pty Ltd

The Drain Man is a business that cleans and relines drains. It falls within the plumbing industry sector. The business owner came to me for help with growing his team, business planning and financial and time management. His circumstances were not uncommon – he was a plumber who lacked business experience and confidence to grow his business. Here are his answers to the questions I asked him, so that we can share his story with you.

1. At what point did you recognise that you needed help, and what motivated you to get it?

I recognised the potential of my business and I had the desire to grow it but did not have the education to put the required structure in place. I hadn't met anyone I felt comfortable talking to in confidence about this until I met Stefan.

2. What did you learn that helped you solve these problems?

I am still learning now – the business is still growing and evolving. The most important thing I have learnt is patience. I learnt to ask questions – play dumb and dig deep. Ask the right questions at the right time of the right people…

I then learnt that business is about the numbers and that without a clear understanding of the numbers you cannot be successful.

3. What systems have you put in place that have helped your business?

I have now put several systems in place to streamline my business:

- Monthly, weekly and daily scoreboard checks on various numbers both financial and operational.
- Utilisation measurement – how to get more done without needing more resources.
- OH&S policies and procedures.

- Training of our people – both skills and attitude.
- Scripts and training for different conversations the staff have with customers.
- Automation of the business to remove duplication.

4. What was the biggest single change you made to yourself or your business that helped turn things around?

I recognised that Stefan was the business coach I needed. I became more accountable and worked on myself to improve as a leader. The business became more professional in everything it did. When Stefan started working with me and my business the demand to improve started. I was doing business out of the kitchen and dining room of my two-bedroom flat. The kitchen bench was my desk!!!

It was late 2007 when I met Stefan. By May 2008 I had leased commercial premises in the same suburb I lived in. We had moved the business into business premises – the mindset had changed for ever…some of the existing staff deselected themselves in various manners and it was clear that they were only working in my business to suit themselves. It was about *them* not the business. I knew this and it was with Stefan's help that we worked this through.

5. What other changes have you made and how have they helped?

We created structure in the business with people (recruitment) in clearly defined roles to allow the business to become less reliant on me.

There was a whole range of things done over the journey and they are still changing as we grow and evolve.

This is one thing that I have maintained throughout the journey – it would have been very easy to say that I have learnt enough and not have Stefan as consultant to the business any longer to save costs. However, it is my position that the complete opposite is the true situation.

Key people are vitally important to the success of a business. This, in turn, means that my team are gold. They need attention and support. Team growth is one thing we have allocated massive resources to.

6. What fears or challenges did you have to overcome? How did you do this?

No fears – that word is not in my vocab. Challenges. The business grew very quickly between 2008 and 2011. Too quickly for my growth. Without Stefan I am sure that it would have been a runaway train destined for a destructive end. However, that has made me grow quicker as the leader.

Sheer determination is how I did it. Never, ever give up. When the going gets tough the tough need to get tougher and ride the bumps. You need to be resilient and have confidence in your own ability and know that you have the support of the people who surround you.

7. What advice do you have for other small business owners who are currently struggling?

Look at yourself and ask yourself first – "How can I improve? What can I do to get better at growing my team?"

Then you need a business coach – and that would be Stefan. But do not expect Stefan to fix all your issues – he can only help you to help yourself. There are no miracle cures here – it is a lot of hard work and persistence.

My only other advice would be, if you are not up for the fight, get out!

8. How is your business performing now? Has this exceeded your expectations?

The business is now much stronger than it has ever been and it is going to get stronger and stronger as we get better at strategy. No, my expectation will never be exceeded – I am a relentless person who will never be happy resting on my laurels. We set goals now and I am just beginning to learn how to dream! This is an interesting concept. I am very proud of my team and our achievements, but will always raise the bar to continue the growth.

9. What specific goals in $ terms have you achieved from implementing the changes you have made?

We have set turnover targets that started back at $10,000 per month and we now consistently exceed $350,000 – it is becoming an expectation – a benchmark.

We have set goals to increase our utilisation[†] – the goal is to get it up over 85%. We started at below 60%. We had 11 staff in the office at the start of 2011 – we now have 5 internals. Utilisation is such an exciting concept – making more with the same or less!!! Our profit goal is growing as our turnover grows. There is no point in turning over more money without profit – that is a useless exercise!

10. What specific non-monetary goals have you achieved?

Growing my team. The change in my team is enormous.
A change in strategy to build more relationships with organisations that require our services on a regular basis –
we are now a B2B business as well as a B2C business.

11. What changes do you still need to make to your business, and why?

We need to get better at finance and time management. We need to grow our strategic alliances. We need to plan better. We need to continue to grow our people.

[†] Utilisation is *return on assests*.

Sales ÷ Assets = Effectiveness of use of assets

Assets = Time, people, machines, etc.

Across your business, how much billable time and resources do you have in a given week that you can sell? If you calculate that you have $10,000 worth of billable assets and your business is earning $6,000 per week, your utilisation rate is 60%, which means there's room for improvement. Good businesses operate at 80%, and the gap between 80% and 100% is where your business becomes a diamond. This figure is a measurement of how well you are turning billable resources into sales.

12. Where do you think your business will be in five years time?

I think we'd have a greater market share with strategic alliances providing 70% of the work. We will have acquired at least two competitors. Our commercial premises will be owned by the company superannuation fund. We will have a band of loyal, raving fans. Perhaps we will expand interstate in Sydney and/or Adelaide?

13. If you hadn't made an effort to get help, where do you think you would be right now?

I'd be on Struggle Street – I shudder to think. Living below the line… a victim… a slave to my business…

14. What are your top five tips for other business owners?

Get involved in Board of Directors 12. Become more accountable. Find your USP and refine it. Find A-grade people and grow them. Dare to dream by finding harmony.

15. How has turning your business around improved your life?

In 2007 I was single, living for work, renting and I did not have an exit strategy. I am now married with four children, working to enjoy life, I own my own home and I am learning to dream which involves my exit strategy.

16. What big goal have you recently achieved in your business?

We have implemented the automation process in the office. The business is now even less reliant on me – that is massive!!!!

17. What big goal have you recently achieved in your life?

To have more time with my beautiful wife!!!

Part 2: Cut

After reading Part 1 you should be starting to develop a strong idea about how to achieve clarity in your business and realise how important this is for your success. We're now going to start looking at what shape your business is going to take; that is, the **cut** of your business.

Like businesses, diamonds come in all sorts of different shapes and cuts. Is your diamond going to be round, or square, or oval. Diamonds can even be shaped like a pear or a heart, and the cuts come with fancy names like 'radiant', 'marquise' and 'asscher'. Like a business, the cut of a diamond can have a significant effect on its value.

Imagine if you were cutting a diamond: you wouldn't start hacking into it and then think about what shape it was going to be! Imagine the mess you'd make! And the money you'd waste! Your business is no different. If you're going to take your business from deadwood to diamond you need to know, before you get started, what cut you are aiming for because every decision you make along the way has to take you in that direction.

After deciding on your desired cut, you then have to put plans and systems in place that ensure this is the cut you end up with. If you don't do this you can decide you want to be a round cut but end up being an oval or a square, or even worse, an unrecognisable mess that's no good to anybody. Every decision you make, every system you put in place, every person you hire, every product or service you offer has to take into consideration what cut you are ultimately trying to achieve. It's not enough just to know the destination; you have to put plans in place to make sure you get there.

So let's find out how you do that.

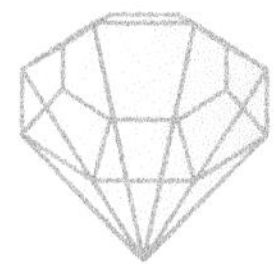

7. IDENTIFYING YOUR DESIRED TARGET MARKET AND MARKET SHARE

When you decide to go into business you need to be absolutely clear about who will buy your product and why. You need to be able to identify them with great clarity. If you are opening a bookshop it's no good just to say, 'I expect booklovers and students to buy my books. I know there are plenty of them out there so I'll be fine.' There's no room for vagueness, guessing, crossing fingers or hopeful estimations when it comes to this stuff. Remember Brendan from earlier in the book? When he first opened his store the extent of his strategic planning was: lots of people come into the city, lots of people like coffee, so if I open a nice coffee shop in the city I should be fine. That's not great market research. In fact, that *isn't* market research, but you'd be surprised how often businesses get started like this. You won't be surprised to know they don't last long if they don't wake up real fast.

If you are in business, or starting a business, you obviously have a product or service that you think other people or organisations want to buy. But *thinking* this and *knowing how* and *why* it will happen are two very different things. At some point in their busy lives, with all sorts of other options available to them, you want people to look at your product and say, 'Yes, this is what I need'. These people or organisations are referred to as your **target market**, and you need to know *exactly* who they are.

Why is this so important? Because if you're not shaping your business from the foundations up, focusing on how you can serve your target market, you are going to try to be everything to everyone and actually be no good to anybody. From a strategic point of view, your desired target market directs the cut of your business.

SO, WHO ARE THEY?

So now that you know why it's so important to find out who your target market is, let's have a look at how you go about doing it.

There are six questions you must be able to answer about your target market. If you can't answer all of these questions you won't be able to cut your business so that it meets the needs of your target market and you'll be left sitting in a quiet room wondering why the phone never rings.

These six questions are:

1. **Who** is the person or organisation you wish to serve? You need to be able to define them in detail. For example, 'parents' is not a well defined target market. What age are they? How many kids do they have?

Where do they live? How much money do they earn? Are they married? Are they single? Defining 'parents' as a target market is just the beginning.

2. **Where** do they congregate in their greatest concentration? Where are they being influenced?

3. **What** is their #1 Big Outcome? What is the problem you solve for them?

4. **When** is their highest level of frustration? When will they say, 'I need to buy this from you'? One in 10 of your future clients is not ready to buy right now but is thinking about doing so. When do they say 'now is the time'?

5. **Why** will they choose you? Why will they discriminate in your favour and open their wallets for you? This is one of the hardest questions to answer. Whatever your product or service, your potential clients have other options available to them. Your challenge is to ensure you get the sale, not your competitors. Your challenge is to ensure you make it easy for them to buy from you.

6. **How** do you expect them to do business with you? How do you expect them to communicate with you, contact you, correspond with you? How can they let you know they are interested in your services? Will this be online, face to face, over the phone, or a combination? In our modern, highly connected world it's more important than ever to make it easy for people to interact with you and buy from you. There are always other businesses they can buy from if you make life hard. How can you let them know about you and your service or product?

The more you understand the who, where, what, when, why and how of your target market the better you'll be able to shape the cut of your business.

HOW MANY OF THEM ARE THERE?

The answers to the above questions will tell you the type of people you are aiming at but they won't tell you how many of them there are. To establish the size of your target market you now need to define what area you are going to target. This can range from local to global and anything in between. For example, a fruit shop can be highly successful just focusing on people in the target market in surrounding suburbs, but this is not likely to work for a carpet cleaner. People buy fruit weekly but only have their carpets cleaned occasionally, so the carpet cleaner would need to focus on an entire city to have a large enough target market. An accounting firm with 20 staff might service the whole of Australia, and a firm with 250 staff might work globally. It's about focusing on a market that is appropriate to the scale of your business – there's no right or wrong answer. For some it's the eastern suburbs, for some it's Melbourne or Perth or Adelaide, or a particular rural region. For some it's the whole of Australia and for some it's global. And it might change over time as you grow. I started off targeting Australia and now I operate globally. This is fine as long as it's part of your strategic growth plan and not random, disorganised expansion just for the sake of it.

It is up to you, before you start to grow, to understand three crucial things about your target market:

◆ How big is it?
◆ What market share do you currently have?

- What market share would you like to have and in what timeframe?

Most business plans fail because business owners miss this step. They simply have a 'gut feeling' or experience in the industry or just wild dreams that tell them willing customers are out there. But to succeed and grow you need to be proactive, certain and precise. You need to get the numbers to make good decisions in your business. And let me make something clear for you right here: whatever your type of business, this information *is available*. You might be able to buy existing market research, and you can certainly do some yourself or pay to have it done. There's no excuse for not being able to answer these questions. If you can't it is not because the information isn't available; it is because you haven't done the work required. This is crucial, factual information that you need to be fully aware of, otherwise you are building your business on the random hope that someone out there at some time might buy from you because you have an awesome product. That's a great plan for a deadwood business. (It's time once again to be brutally honest with yourself. Are you going to do this or not?)

GOING DEEPER: NICHES

Once you've answered all these questions and begun to identify and break down your target market, guess what? It's time to do it again! That's right, your target market can be further broken down into niches that will help give you even more clarity about your customers and how you can end their frustration.

Once you have answered the above questions with confidence and clarity, have a look at the market you have defined and see how you can break it down even further. For example, my broader target market is business owners ranging from start-ups to $5 million businesses. Within this there are all sorts of niches that I can target separately, such as trades, professional services, manufacturing, retail, hospitality, entertainment and arts. As a broad category they all fall into my target market, but have a think about each niche and the questions we posed above. By refining and identifying these niches I can improve my focus even further.

And even within these niches there are further vertical markets you can target; for example, within trades you have plumbers, electricians, carpenters, plasterers, tilers, roofers, and on and on it goes. Within professional services we have doctors, lawyers, accountants, architects and much more. You can even break doctors down into chiropractors, physios, GPs, oncologists, podiatrists, surgeons and cardiologists. The high-level categories are very useful, but once you break it down even further you'll really be able to identify with clarity and confidence who your target market is, why they buy from you and how you can reach them. In my business, when I really want to focus what I'm doing I might spend a whole quarter just focusing on, for example, chiros.

The Drain Man – who you met in the previous case study – is a great example of finding a niche. They are registered plumbers, but they just clear and reline drains. That's it. They don't do taps or hot water or showers. It's just like a brain surgeon compared to a GP – they are plumbers with specialist solutions. The industry is plumbing but the niche is drain-clearing.

While the overall #1 Big Outcome might be the same for an architect and a physio – say, to increase business by 100% in 12 months – how they each go about it will be different, so this allows me to tailor offers even more specifically to meet these clients' needs. Will the architect and the physio read the same industry magazines, attend the same events and have the same colleagues? Not likely. So my marketing has to be different. What is the investment vs ROI for each? What are their frustrations and their freedoms? When will they buy from me? While their goals may be broadly similar, everything my business does can be refined to better meet the needs of these two different businesses, thereby increasing the chances that they will purchase from me and not my competitors.

Each one of the niches you identify needs to be defined and dissected, just like your overall target market. You need to ask the who, where, what, when, why and how questions again, then identify its size, how much of it you currently have and how much of it you would like to have in what timeframe. This is the start of creating your marketing plan with clarity and confidence and turning your business into a well-oiled machine. Who are you building this business for? What is the cut? The underlying foundation? If you don't know who these people are and what they want, the only way you can solve their problems is by getting lucky, and luck is not a solid business fundamental or a strategy for success.

COST OF GROWTH VS COST OF OPPORTUNITY

We all know that there are going to be costs involved in taking your business to the next level. How you approach those costs will be pivotal to whether your business goes to the next phase or languishes where it is now.

There are two different mindsets you can have when you look at costs: you can see them as the **cost of growth** or the **cost of opportunity**.

Let me explain.

Being in cost of growth mode means having a short-term outlook and seeing everything purely in terms of dollars spent. You have an *expense* mindset. You look at each decision and say, 'Geez, I'm not sure I can afford that right now,' without looking further into the future and recognising the long-term benefits of spending that money. When you are in cost of growth mode you are holding yourself back and limiting your horizons.

When you look at decisions as opportunities and not simply costs, your whole horizon will expand. You are clear about where you are going and you are moving forward within the market that you are targeting. You are reaching out and grabbing the opportunity, rather than letting your fears hold you back. You have an *investment* mindset.

Let's have a look at an example. Let's say you run a retail outlet and you are considering expanding to a larger store as business has been good and you think you are on the right track. If you are in cost of growth mode, you'll do all your sums and decide that maybe it doesn't quite add up. Maybe you're not ready after all. Maybe you don't have the financial resources to pull it off right now. You might next year, but not now. Or maybe you think your current little store is where you belong. Maybe you're not willing to go to the edge of the cliff.

But if you are moving forward with clarity and confidence, you will not see expansion in a new location as a cost but as an opportunity. You'll understand what the new location will bring – it will make everything bigger and better and launch the next phase of your business.

Perhaps the decision will hurt you in the short term, whether it's your finances, your operations – whatever. But sometimes you must go two steps backwards to go four steps forward. If you're in cost of growth mode you'll just see the two steps back, but if you're in cost of opportunity mode you'll also see the four steps forward. This is how you grow a business. It's not a licence to throw money at something every chance you get, but it is about being bold and backing yourself if you've put in the hard yards.

 ## CHAPTER GEMS

- When you decide to go into business you need to be absolutely clear about who will buy your product and why.

- There are six questions you must be able to answer about your target market: who, where, what, when, why, how?

- Your target market can then be further broken down into niches that will help give you even more clarity about your customers.

- Do you have an expense mindset or an investment mindset? You can only have one of the two. It may be time to consider a long-term change if you wish to go from deadwood to diamond.

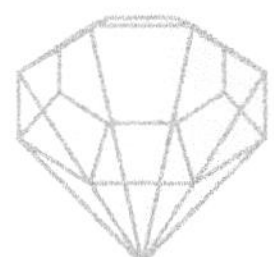

8. IS YOUR TREE DYING OR GROWING?

Your business grows just a little bit or dies just a little bit every single day. That's right. Every day. It's never standing still. Today it is just a little bit stronger or a little bit weaker than it was yesterday. This is something not a lot of business owners think about as they get caught up in the day-to-day craziness of just trying to keep work and money coming in the door.

So is *your business* growing or dying? Is it stronger or weaker than it was yesterday, or the day before? Or a month ago, or a year? If you are reading this book, chances are the trend is downward. But that's okay! Don't despair! I've met people with a tree they were ready to chop down and use for firewood because they thought it was well and truly dead, but with the right help we've been able to nurture it back to full health. It's about having the right ethos and the right mindset to execute the right strategies and follow through. If you've thrown your hands up in the air and said 'It's dead!', well, then it is, because with that attitude you're never going to get anywhere. Even if you do want to turn things around, if you're okay with mediocrity and sitting around waiting for things to happen things won't get better. To reverse the fortunes of a tree that's dying it takes determination and an attitude of this *has to happen*. It's about making and taking opportunities, it's about growing yourself and your business and those around you.

Your business is either growing or dying – there's no in between.

If you don't keep moving forward, nurturing and challenging, the focus of your business will always be where your original purpose was. The cut of your business at its humble beginnings will be your strength. If you have a strong operational arm at the beginning this will come through. A plumber who has excellent plumbing skills but not much else will have a very strong operational arm but not be very good at sales, marketing, finance and so on. A business can be started like that but it can't be grown like that.

So how do you make sure your business is growing rather than dying? To make sure you are not going backwards each day you have to find out where your weaknesses are, because these are the areas that are holding you back. If you don't take the time to stop and figure out what these are, your business is getting weaker every day, probably without you knowing why.

How does your business rate in the four key strategic areas of sales, marketing, operations and finance? Most businesses are strong at one, or maybe two, of these and they muddle through with the rest. If your business is going to survive and then thrive, it needs to be strong in each of these areas.

What is the cut of your business right now? Score your business out of 10 for each area. Maybe your business has great operations and has managed to struggle through on this basis, but your sales, marketing and finance are hopeless and only get done when people can squeeze them in. This is a common problem and it doesn't get better by itself.

The Strategic Tetrahedron

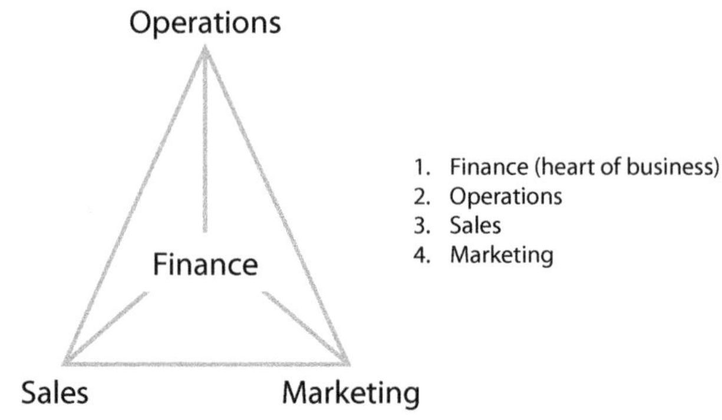

In these four key strategic areas your business must continue to run at a better level every day, and for this to happen you must be strategically aware of where the gaps are in performance. At the start there will always be gaps because resources are limited and you don't know what you don't know, but once you move out of the start-up phase there is no excuse for not being strong in all of these areas. Remember, if your business isn't growing every day it's dying.

EXERCISE: The Strategic Tetrahedron

Rate yourself out of 10 in each of these four areas. What could you do to improve your rating by one point in each of these areas in the next 90 days?

Finance: _______ /10

I can improve this by: ____

____

____

Operations: _______ /10

I can improve this by: ____

____

____

Sales: _______ /10

I can improve this by: ____

____

____

Marketing: _______ /10

I can improve this by: ____

____

____

You can't have one of these key areas ahead of the others because the weak links will hold you back. It becomes a choke point. It doesn't matter how good your operations are if your invoicing is hopeless and it takes ages for the money to come in. That's not the way to growth. And it doesn't matter if your finances are fantastic if your operations are poor, because nobody will buy from you so there will be nobody to invoice. How do you raise capital? How do you market your business? How do you close sales? How do you manage your finances? How do your operations run? Like a tree, everything has to work together and grow together. If you don't nourish a tree and look after it, it will die. Your business is no different. Don't let the choke points kill it through indifference or inattention.

Note that I haven't said *you* need to be strong in each of these areas. We've already discussed the need for great staff and the value of outsourcing. Don't think that you personally need to become an accountant or a marketing manager. While it's essential for you to be aware of everything, you don't need to be the *expert* at everything – and in fact, you can't be! There simply aren't enough hours in the day. So get rid of the Lone Ranger attitude that too many small business owners have and get some help. A business that doesn't have good processes in place and is okay with mediocrity will have trouble attracting good staff. If I'm a worker, do I want to work with a small business with no plans or a business that is going somewhere? Growth must be a fundamental part of all aspects of your business.

Look at yourself, your business and your life like a tree that's growing and needs constant nurturing. If you see branches that are starting to whither that's a sign of trouble and you have to act now. The survival of your business may depend on it.

How's your tree going?

HAVING THE DISCIPLINE TO FOLLOW THROUGH

An important part of the cut of your business is discipline and determination. Part of your DNA – and that of your staff – needs to be having an attitude of doing whatever it takes. People naturally gravitate towards doing things they love or enjoy, but sometimes in business you need to get your hands dirty and learn things and do things that may not float your boat. Hey, that's why it's called work. You can't just have the road map; the rubber has to hit the road at some point for you to get anywhere.

When you have created a strategic plan and are clear about your target market and why they should choose you, you have to be confident in your plan and you have to push through. Sometimes it's two steps backwards to go four steps forward, and that's okay. This stuff can be hard, but it's your responsibility to create and build the business with clarity. As the business leader it's up to you to – LEAD! If you're not leading, nobody is following. You don't have to do everything yourself, but you do need to set the example for everybody in your business to follow. You need to see the choke point before it happens, not the day before but weeks or months before. It's your responsibility to solve the problem, to do the things you are good at and let others do the things they are good at. People won't follow you just because you're the boss, they'll follow you because they respect you, they can see your determination and desire, and they want the business to do well. It's about achieving the common goal. It's all about accountability being part of the DNA of your business. It's about a focus on doing the little things well. Saying 'I'll get around to it later' just won't do. Your finances won't get better by themselves, but they will get worse. Your target customers won't land on your doorstep and introduce themselves; you have to go to them. Your clients won't close their own sales. You have to keep growing your strengths and building on your weaknesses and get something to show for each day in accordance with your plan.

Laser focus to break through to continuous success

Just like an elite sportsperson you are either in the zone and not easily distracted or you're not; you have the required determination or you don't; you have ownership, accountability and responsibility or you don't. This is most important when it comes to focus. Do you have the laser focus on what you need to achieve that will keep you on track?

We all know what it's like to start the day with a long list of things to do. At 9 am it looks a bit long but you think you'll get through it okay. By 10.27 am you've crossed off only one thing because you've spent all your time fixing problems that you should really be leaving to other people. By 4.15 pm you've only crossed off three things, and – as you did yesterday – you move the remaining items to tomorrow's list. Because, you know, tomorrow will be different, right?

Of course tomorrow won't be different – so *you* have to be different. It is definitely not okay to have your business focus diluted. The first thing you can do is shorten your things-to-do list drastically. You should only have three or four key things to achieve each day. Remember, you're outsourcing, delegating or terminating the less important stuff, aren't you? You should be using the **DOTS Options** we looked at earlier. If you are doing too much at once – such as having many more projects on the go than you can handle or trying to wear every single hat in the business – and you are not getting help, you will get the results you deserve, and they won't be good. You need to be clear about the three vital things that need to be achieved today to get you closer to your goals, not the 50 things that are on your to-do list that will allow you to tick a box but not really contribute to your long-term success.

The second key to getting through the important things each day is to do the toughest things first. Most people naturally avoid the things they don't want to do, so they pile up and keep getting put off until tomorrow. This keeps happening day after day, so that some things never get done at all. So, each day, look at your list and see what important thing on it you *least* want to do and do that first. This will stop you getting distracted, it will stop the procrastination. This approach has been called *eating the frog*[#]. If you'd rather stick a fork in your eye than make some marketing phone calls, do these calls first. You'll feel better after they are done and you'll be able to get on with your day. And they won't be as bad as you think anyway – things never are. Success often comes from breaking out of your comfort zone, so make it happen!

Having your day well planned and well structured is hugely important in helping your business move forward. How you manage your day got you where you are now and you're not happy with that, so clearly things need to change. I know what I'm doing each day from the moment I walk through the door. I have everything scheduled, including time for dealing with unplanned issues that arise. When I'm in the middle of an important task the phone and the email are ignored and, unless they are urgent, any problems are

---

[#] This is a technique shared by Brian Tracy, personal development guru.

ignored. I keep that laser focus until the task is complete. I'm at the gym by 6.05 am every day, not because I don't get much done but because my days are well planned, I have the focus to stick to the plan, and I don't waste my time on things that are unimportant or that I'm not good at. This didn't just happen. It's a direct result of my approach to each and every day. Like everybody, I get the results I deserve.

I've had new clients come to me who look like they haven't slept in a month. They explain to me how they are working 15-hour days and they always seem to be busy, but somehow this isn't showing up in the bank account. So what's going on here? These people are confusing activity with productivity, a common problem among small business owners. If this sounds like you there are two things you need to look at: you are probably spending your time doing a lot of unproductive tasks that keep you running around but don't move the business forward, or you might not be charging enough so you're working below your real value. Or, if things are a real mess, you might be doing both.

Don't let yourself get to the stage of being desperate and dateless, where you'll say yes to anything and end up working for $12 an hour. This starts a downward spiral that leads to bad decisions which compound over time, and you end up with a business so lacking in direction and focus that you barely know what you should be doing when you arrive at the office. When trouble looms on the horizon, tackle it head on, immediately.

There will be periods of doubt and there will be negative self-talk. Am I going about this the right way? Have I been brutally honest about what the opportunity is and how I will realise it? How high does that peak look? Am I owning it? Certain points on the journey will be lonely and scary, and you will need commitment and focus to persevere. You're not going to come up with a plan in five minutes. You need laser focus.

Think about a pilot starting out on a flight from Melbourne to London. That plane needs to be lined up to the centimetre at a specific gate 17,000 kilometres away so that the doors can open safely and the passengers can disembark. Does the pilot start lining up at that gate in London when he's leaving the gate in Melbourne? Of course not. There are hundreds of steps he has to take in between before he gets to that far away gate. First, he has to taxi out to the right runway, then he has to take off safely, then he has to reach the right speed and altitude, and there are stopovers along the way. He takes the plane to Bangkok or Singapore and then hands it over to another pilot. The destination is still London. All of these are small steps that are carefully planned with the one aim of getting to that gate at Heathrow. It doesn't matter if the flight gets a little off course here and there, due to the weather for example; the pilot will adjust as the journey continues and the ultimate goal isn't affected. The pilot can do this because he knows his destination. If the pilot wasn't sure whether he was flying to London or New York, he wouldn't know what decisions to make along the way to keep himself on course. Throughout the flight he has laser focus on his destination. Each of his stopovers allows him to get back on track so minor variations in the journey don't affect the final outcome.

This is how you must run your business. If you don't know where it's headed, how will you keep it on track? How will you even know if you're going in the right direction? You must master a deep-seated commitment to where you are going.

Get this sorted and it's game on.

GO SLOW TO GO FAST

You will see a massive increase in tempo when you start doing this stuff well. Good things will start happening all around you. You'll start attracting new customers, your marketing will get a good response, you'll be closing sales, your finances will start to improve. It's very exciting when you start to see your hard work pay off. This is a great sign that you are on the right track.

It is, however, just as important to maintain your focus and discipline when this happens. It's not time to get overexcited and think you've made it, that you've found the secret to success and your future is assured. This is just the first step. When this flurry of activity starts you must make sure you are still doing the critical few things to keep your business strong, not the trivial many things that have little or no noticeable effect on your business outcomes. You have to slow down and assess what this extra activity means for your business and how you will manage it. This is a great chance to start automating, delegating and outsourcing, so you can start turning your business into a sleek and efficient machine that purrs along with no excess baggage.

What do your customers want from you? You can't give them everything because you are not ready yet, so don't get ahead of yourself. Focus on what you can do for them now and do this as well as you can. It can be too easy when this excitement kicks in to try to race to the finish line. It can be tempting to try to grow ahead of the plan, or to spend more money, or to recruit new staff that maybe aren't really needed. Don't release that 15-page menu if it's not ready. Don't open another location just because this one is booming. Stick to your plan.

Here's a great example of how even established and successful companies can lose focus. You've no doubt heard of cloud computing. It's where your files and information, and sometimes your software as well, are stored on the internet, or 'in the cloud' as it's called. A few years ago IT companies could see that the cloud was going to be the next big thing so they were all trying to get their products out first. Apple's offering was called MobileMe. It was a service that allowed people to store photos, music, documents, emails and all sorts of other stuff in the cloud, so that they could access it from anywhere on any device. Or, at least, that's what it was *supposed* to do. But the email service crashed, files didn't sync properly, it was difficult to set up, and some of the services simply didn't work. And this from the company renowned for producing exquisitely designed and executed products that simply did what they were supposed to do.

So how did a company as esteemed as Apple get it so wrong? They didn't slow down to go fast. They saw a big opportunity in front of them and they went for it without having the resources to do it properly. Steve Jobs later said: 'It was a mistake to launch MobileMe at the same time as iPhone 3G, iPhone 2.0 software and the App Store. We all had more than enough to do, and MobileMe could have been delayed without consequence.' Instead of executing a carefully thought-out strategic plan, they dived in head first. If you know your destination, have a strategic plan in place and you stick to it with laser focus, you will avoid these temptations to try to short-cut success that instead most often lead to failure. MobileMe was shut down after just three years. Apple's visionary leader Steve Jobs said, 'It wasn't our finest hour'.

Slowing down and putting the right systems in place will mean you later go faster than you could ever have imagined. Being smooth makes you go fast. Being well organised makes you go fast. Making good decisions makes you go fast. Running around trying to do 100 things at once does not make you go fast. You must go slow to go fast. This is a significant part of the cut of the business. It's no good being in a frantic rush to get to the finish line and then crashing at the last turn because your business is a collection of hastily assembled systems and rushed decisions held together with wishful thinking. A careful and systematic approach must be part of the DNA of your business.

Slow things down so that everyone in your organisation is focused on the critical few and not the trivial many. Don't confuse activity with production. Be focused on your goal and follow through with discipline. Know what your stopovers are along the way and use them to assess where you are going and what you can do to stay on track. You are not going slow because you are fearful. You are going slow because you are confident.

Remember: **Get brilliant at the basics.**

BORED AND RICH VS EXCITABLE AND BROKE

You may have started your own business because you thought it would be exciting. You'd be making quick and big decisions, being responsible for success or failure, flying by the seat of your pants.

Not me. Don't get me wrong, I like excitement as much as the next guy. I'm going to have my first experience on a car racing track later this year and I can't wait. I like to travel and do all sorts of other fun stuff. But that's not why I go to work. I want to be bored at work. That's right, bored. I want to be so bored that an email from my accountant is the highlight of my day. Bored, bored, bored. Bored. Get it? Bored.

Now, I know right now you're thinking, what on earth is he on about? Why does *anybody* want to be bored. Here's why. I want my staff and I to be so focused on our products and goals that it's boring. I want things to be so well planned that it's boring. I want my business to run so smoothly that it's boring. I want us to stay committed with clarity and concentrate on the one thing that we are best known for, so that nothing distracts us.

I've seen plenty of businesses that seem like exciting places to work, and maybe they are – while they are still around. Hastily called meetings, endless problem-solving, racing for deadlines, things almost but not quite working out, having to constantly be ready for the next emergency – it *can* be exciting. But it *won't* be profitable. If you want excitement take up hang gliding, motorbike riding or mountain climbing. Travel the world. Go diving. These are things you'll be able to afford to do when your stable and boring business starts bringing in the cash and freeing up your time.

You want a great example of boring? How about Coke? It's quite a boring product when you think about it. A black fizzy drink in a red can, among many other fizzy drinks in cans. But Coke knows who its target market is and how to reach it, and it keeps doing the same things over and over again. People buy Coke because of the reputation it has, not because it's an exciting product.

If you are not testing and measuring to get better at what you do you will be excitable and broke. If you don't know who your target market is and how to reach it you will constantly jump from one idea to the next without knowing what will or won't work. Magic fixes and shiny things will look good and might get people interested for five minutes but they will cause you to go broke real quick.

Have a laser focus on your target market. Figure out what your business does well and do it over and over again. Build a reputation for being great at one thing. Be boring. You've heard of a multi-pronged attack? You need to be a one-pronged attack. Create your plan and then stick to it with clarity and confidence. Don't jump at the latest fads. Don't do anything stupid because you think you need to be successful tomorrow. I used to run five businesses at once because I thought that was the way to success. I thought I was being smart, and it sure was exciting. Now I run one business very well, rather than five with no idea what is going on. Which approach do you think has been more successful?

ADDING MORE ZEROS TO THE HOURLY RATE

In the clarity section we discussed what you could do if you added a zero to your hourly rate. What would it mean for your business if you were working for $1,000 an hour for just one hour a week, instead of $100? It's an exciting prospect. But now have a think about this: what would it mean for your business if *all of your staff* could do this?

This is a concept that you can apply to all of your people throughout your business. It's not just for you or your management team. Part of deciding on, and creating the cut of, your business is about getting the most out of your staff, about making things run more smoothly and putting systems in place. As you do this you will be able to find one hour a week for each of your team members when they can think *big*, when they can let go of worrying about the normal responsibilities of their job and really go for it. What can each staff member do to help your business hit it out of the park? What big idea can they come up with that will make your business more efficient, or help you find new clients, or help you close more sales? I know you have lots of talented and hard-working people around you, because you would remove anybody who wasn't. So let them off the leash. Allow them to dream and think large.

If you want your staff to fully realise their potential it has to start with you. If you think small and lack confidence, so will your staff. But if you show them how to break free and take a chance and walk to the edge of the cliff, if this is how you run your company, they will follow you. It's about coaching and mentoring them. It's about giving them strategies so they can excel. It's about creating an environment in your business that encourages and rewards initiative, lateral thinking and effort. If you're not leading your staff won't follow. If you haven't got this right for yourself you can't expect your staff to get it right.

Not only will this help boost your business results now, it will help you attract and retain the best talent which helps boost your business over the longer term. Nobody wants to work for a business that is stuck in the mud, especially talented and dedicated people. They want to work at a company where they will be inspired, where they will be encouraged to have input and be allowed to learn and grow. A business like yours, right?

You've done it for yourself, now do it for your team. You don't need them to work more, you need them to work more effectively and efficiently. If you have the right people, soon they'll be able to complete their tasks better than you can – and that's great! You want to be surrounded by people who are better at things than you are. Then you can give them more responsibilities and free yourself up to focus on growing the business. This is an important foundation for growth.

BELIEF

It has to be non-negotiable that you will get up at 7 am, or 6 am, or even 5 am, every day so that you can do what you need to do to make your tree grow. You have to simply take it for granted that this will happen, that you will do *whatever it takes*. You must expect and demand it of yourself.

If it were easy everybody would be doing it. Right now all of your friends and family would be running million-dollar businesses, driving fancy cars and going on holidays every other month. But it's not easy. We know this. So you need to be brutally honest with yourself and have a true inner belief that you will do whatever it takes to succeed. Sometimes you will feel like you are the only person who can push through, and if you do others will follow you. But if you have a belief that you can't, others will follow this as well.

When you tap into your purpose you become bullet-proof. The strongest muscle in the body is the brain, so program your purpose into your brain. It influences everything. Belief and purpose will help you through. It starts and finishes with the faith to believe.

Ultimately your **beliefs** are a by-product of your **values**. What is your hierarchy of values? What is *non-negotiable* for you that you are transferring to your business? What is acceptable and what is not acceptable for how you treat staff and your customers? What about trust and honesty? What about effort?

Values are a by-product of your **identity** and who you really are. Are you playing a bigger game than what is really going on? Are you pretending? Are you hiding from the brutal truth? Do you appear externally excited but you're dying inside? Are you not recognising that you've come a long way and you are more advanced than you think? How do you truly understand your relationships with your suppliers and customers? How do you see yourself as a business?

To go one step further, your identity was forged by the **environment** you were brought up in as a young child and a younger adult. The ability and confidence to believe in yourself and that you can achieve was something that came to you at a very young age. It's about tapping into your inner strength and knowing that you can get the results you want and deserve. You have a responsibility to tap into that every day. Your whole identity needs to be built around belief, resilience, persistence, momentum, tenacity, clarity and follow-through.

Environment also refers to where your business operates today. If you're not clear about the environment you are setting up in, chances are this will be the problem that holds you back. Should your business be operating in the eastern suburbs, or in just one suburb, or throughout the state or the country? If you get this wrong nothing else will work. The identity of your business and everything that follows will be wrong.

Be clear on your environment and your skill-set. This is how you build a business that is going to last a lot longer than you.

Freud believed that most of our conscious behaviour is determined by our unconscious mind. This can be represented like an iceberg. Other business gurus, such as ActionCOACH founder and CEO Brad Sugars, have further developed this idea into what is now known as the Identity Iceberg.

The Identity Iceberg

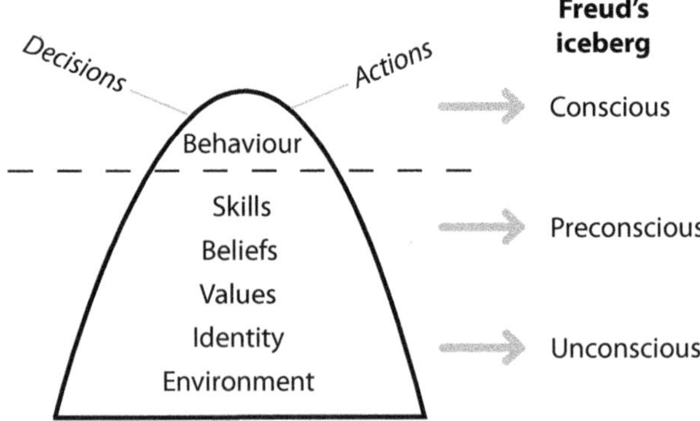

Why is this so important? People can't actually see your beliefs or values or identity, so why do they matter? Have a look at the diagram above. What they *can* see and experience is your **behaviour**. Your beliefs, values and identity are all under the surface. They may go unnoticed. But what most definitely does not go unnoticed are your behaviour and actions, and what people see above the surface is determined by what is going on under the surface. This is known as the **Identity Iceberg.** Your plan starts with your beliefs but what people see is your behaviour. Your results are a by-product of the decisions you make and the actions that you follow through with.

Let's have a look at some examples.

What about a plumber who thinks it's okay to be 20 minutes late to appointments, to leave places in a mess when he's done, to expect people to pay cash so he can avoid tax and to drive around in a grubby car because, well, that's what plumbers do. You can learn a lot about this guy's identity, values and beliefs from these behaviours, and none of it is good.

What about Brendan, who we met earlier? His **identity** was that he was an independent, hard-working entrepreneur. His **values** were that he wanted to serve the best coffee in Melbourne and provide a relaxing environment by engaging with his staff and customers. His unflinching **belief** was that he had what it takes to succeed and that he would be able to open ten stores around the city in the future. His **skills** needed some work in certain areas but he was aware of this and was prepared to learn and also hire the right people when needed. There was nothing wrong with his **behaviour;** he worked hard and did everything he could to make the business a success. This all sounds great – so what went wrong? After two years, why was he entertaining more pigeons than customers? Because his **environment** was wrong. As he had relied on gut instinct he had opened the coffee shop in a poor location, and because of this he was doomed from the start. It didn't matter that he had all the other attributes necessary for success. In the wrong location none of this was going to help. But when he made that one big decision and changed the environment by moving the store, things turned around. The environment for the coffee shop was wrong from day one so he didn't stand a chance if he didn't make some changes.

GROWING YOUR IDENTITY

If you are too far ahead of your identity you are headed for trouble. What does this mean? Well, let's say you are a music promoter and you've just started a business managing and organising concerts. Your first event at the local pub went well, with about 100 people attending (even some who weren't your family or friends) and some good local bands. A good night was had by all and you put some money in the bank. A great start!

So what do you do for a follow up? If your next step is to approach Justin Bieber and tell him you can sell out the MCG, how far do you think you are going to get? Let me tell you: not far at all.

If you are too far ahead of your identity you'll get found out. It's okay to dare to dream, but just for a minute. Then it's time to get back to work. If you get carried away you are going to let people down, and there's nothing worse for the reputation of your business. Your identity needs to be *just* ahead of you; that's how you grow. You'll see the choke points and the speed bumps ahead and be able to navigate them, but you won't bite off more than you can chew.

If you are too far *behind* your identity you are holding yourself back and procrastinating. Maybe you have a voice telling you this is not for you. This can be your subconscious. I say to my clients all the time, 'Get out of your own way. There's a freight train ready to be let loose. It's *you* standing in the way.'

Have a think about what your identity should be for *your* business. Think about your target market, your products and services, your staff, your systems – everything. What should be the identity of your business?

Now, have a think about what the identity of your business *actually is*. Look around you and think about where you are now.

Now compare the two. Is there a gap between where you think you should be and where you are right now? Most business owners would say yes, there is a gap. And I can see you getting a bit worried by this gap, because doesn't it mean you are not performing as well as you should?

No! That's not what it means at all. There should be a gap between where you are and where you think you *should* be – because that's how you keep growing and moving forward. If you ever get to the point where you think your business has achieved everything it can and it is in the perfect position, you're in trouble, because no business ever actually reaches this point. Not mine. Not the multi-billion-dollar behemoths that are listed on the stock exchange. Not the local coffee shop that is always overflowing with customers. There is *always* room for your business to grow and improve and change and adapt. You need to keep nourishing your tree. Remember, if you're not growing you're dying; there is no in between.

Occasionally I have clients who think they have actually overtaken their own identity and grown into something they're not and this can be a real problem. If you think you are ahead of where you actually are you are not being honest with yourself or your clients, and you will get found out very quickly.

Your identity needs to keep growing, like a tree, and if you are going to push your identity forward you need to look hard at your business and be honest with yourself and see where you need to make changes. Once you almost catch up to your identity it's time to move it ahead again to the next phase of your planned strategic growth. Don't hope this is going to happen. Make it happen. Are you playing to your maximum potential and performing at your personal best every day? Are you being reactive or proactive? It's time for some brutal truth questions.

 ## CHAPTER GEMS

- Your business grows just a little bit or dies just a little bit every single day.

- Sometimes it takes two steps backwards to go four steps forward.

- What is the identity of your business? Is it progressive?

- When the flurry of activity starts you must make sure you are still doing the critical few things to keep your business strong.

- It's better to be bored and rich rather than excitable and broke.

- What would it mean for your business if you and your team were working for a x10 hourly rate for just one hour a week?

- If you are too far ahead of your identity you are headed for trouble.

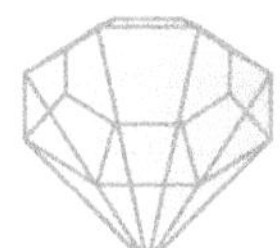

9. GETTING RESULTS

THE QUALITY OF LIFE LADDER

Further to some of the learnings from my mentor Brad Sugars, we're now going to have a look at the Quality of Life Ladder.

The quality of the results you get out of your business is influenced by many things and will ultimately affect your quality of life. If you don't get good results out of your business your quality of life won't be much better. We're now going to look at what is known as the **Quality of Life Ladder** formula, which gives you a process that will lead to great results for your business and a high quality of life for you.

The steps are shown in the diagram overleaf and explained below it. Each step builds on the previous one, so you must start at 1 and work your way up.

The Quality of Life Ladder

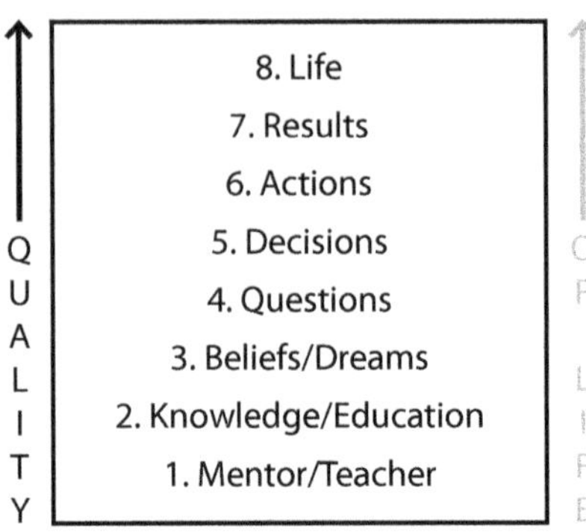

1. Good quality results begin with good quality mentors and teachers. You should be on a path of continuous learning throughout your life. I've had a business coach for as long as I've been in business, because I'm not crazy enough to believe that I know everything or that I have all the answers. I'm very good at what I do and I've been very successful, but there's always more for me to learn. Always. It's also important that you surround yourself with people who support and encourage your dreams. Spend time with dream-makers, not dream-takers.

2. It's vital that you educate yourself thoroughly about business. The quality of knowledge and education you have and strive for will greatly influence your results.

3. The quality of the beliefs and dreams that you have will spur you on. Are you dreaming big? *Really* big? Are you aiming for 200% growth, not 2%? Do you demand success, or is average okay? Goals are great and can help your business move forward, but to truly uncover a diamond you need dreams.

4. The quality of questions you ask will determine the quality of the answers you receive. You need to know what the gaps are in your knowledge and skills and get the right information to fill these gaps. Ask more *how* questions.

5. The quality of the decisions that you strategically make will determine the direction of your business. Get all the information you need and then make confident and clear decisions with your #1 Big Outcome in mind. Know where you are now, where you're going and how you're going to get there. You also need to have 'plan B' thinking. Be prepared for problems before they arise. Anticipate the choke points in your business. Know the worst-case scenarios and have a plan for them, then if they occur you can sit back and laugh as your contingency plan kicks in and you sail on because you were well prepared. You can have focus and discipline because all the strategic thinking has been done.

6. What is the quality of your actions? Are what you *say* you are going to do and what you *actually* do the same? Are you delivering your customers from point A to point B? An attitude of near enough is good enough is a great plan for a deadwood business.

This is all about the cut. You'll notice we're not even talking about money yet, because if you make good quality decisions about the cut of your business and you follow through on your plan with clarity and determination the money will follow. And this ultimately leads to a quality of life that you deserve. We *all* get the quality of life we deserve, whatever that may be.

Ask yourself a brutal truth question: how is your business going to be better tomorrow, next week, next month, next year? It's not just going to magically happen. You have to make it happen. Just go for it. Money comes and goes, but if you're not clear on why you are there you need to get out. You either have a strong purpose or you don't. You either care or you don't. Your attitude must be: *I care and I'll do what it takes and I'll always do the right thing.*

You must ensure that all these steps are in place. This is how you transform to a better quality of life.

SIX PILLARS TO EXCEPTIONAL GROWTH

What you are about to read is the framework for my exclusive Business Fundamentals workshop series; that's how important it is. The **Six Pillars to Exceptional Growth** are the foundations for the success of your business. If you can master these six areas you will have the fundamentals in place for success. Think about that word for a minute: *fundamentals*. This is not about making your business flashy or building an empire. These are the nuts-and-bolts basics without which no business can succeed over the long term. If you don't have confidence and clarity around each of these pillars your business will collapse sooner or later – most likely sooner. It's about predictability for long-term profitability. This is the foundation premise for your business. Get brilliant at the basics. It's about mastery.

The Six Pillars to Exceptional Growth

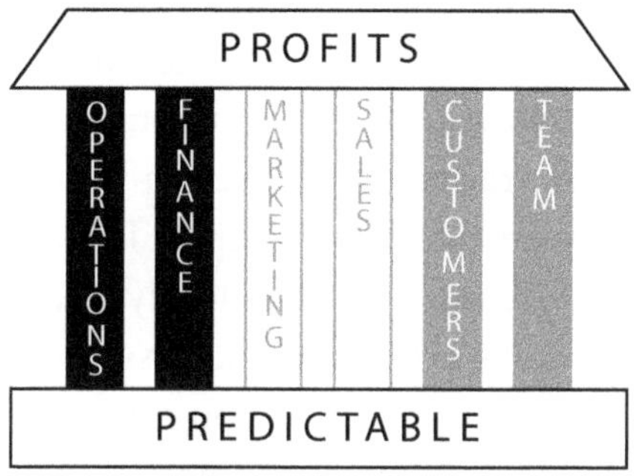

How do you build your business so that it lasts for the long term? You have to be brutally honest with yourself when you rate yourself in each of these areas:

1. **Operations.** Exactly what are you going to do and how do you set it up so it becomes sustainable and systematised? How will you serve your clients? How will they buy from you and how do you deliver? Think about your marketing and your finance, terms of trade, administration and your customer service in general. What about your team development and recruiting? This is where all elements of your business must be predictable and easy to follow. Even businesses that have been operating for many years don't necessarily have the best operations in place. *Every time you grow so do your operations.* You must be preparing for future growth. Operations are ongoing. What are the key things you do in this area?

2. **Finance.** Like sport, business has a scoreboard and you must understand it if you are going to win. That scoreboard is finance. You want brutal honesty about how your business is going? Look at your figures. You

can talk big to your friends and you can tell your clients you've made $7 million so far this year, but your figures don't lie. They are the final scoreboard on all the decisions you've made in your business. If you're figures are strong you've made good decisions, if not you haven't. It's that simple. The three key scoreboards you need to thoroughly understand – in no particular order – are profit and loss, the balance sheet and the cashflow forecast. If you don't continuously look at these and understand finance – which is the language of business – you are in trouble. Business is an intellectual sport. This tells you if you are winning or losing. How are you running your business if you don't speak this language? Imagine a pilot who walks into the cockpit and says, 'Look at all these dials!' Do you look at finance and say, 'What the hell is this?' If so, this needs to be right at the top of your list of problems to remedy. (I have just the workshop for you!) You need to know your break even, gross profit, cost centres as a percentage, and the balance sheet – this is the most important scoreboard of all. It tells you the truth – the cold hard truth – about *every decision you have made in your business to date*. From day 1. Not many people understand that. It's a mirror. Look into it.

3. **Marketing.** For your marketing to get results you must intimately understand three specific areas: your unique selling proposition (USP), your emotional selling proposition (ESP) (connecting with your current and future clients) and your community selling proposition (CSP), for which you are building a reputation from

many of your customers and advocates who are confirming and saying, 'Yes, the product and service you need are here, and they give you just a little bit more'. (Make sure this is just a little bit more, not a lot more. If you are too generous with a client because business is quiet you have set a standard that you can't hope to maintain, and you'll inevitably disappoint this client in the future.) Marketing is 24/7. It's ongoing. It happens looooong before the first sale and waaaaaay after the latest one. You can see how this works in the diagram below. If you build your USP this will help you build your ESP, which will lead to a growth in your CSP, and this provides validation for your USP which allows you to build on it further, which leads to…and on it goes. How's that for a virtuous cycle?

The Selling Proposition Virtuous Cycle

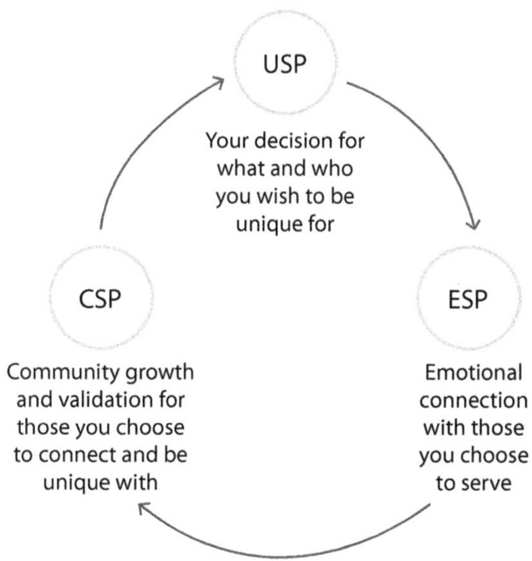

4. **Sales.** If you have generated attention and interest via marketing, now you need a call to action. You need to make it easy to buy from you with a process of multiple steps, so that when people knock on your door you lead them through the process. Remember, your competitors are lurking just around the corner waiting to snap up customers if you make things difficult. Sales is the *only activity* that actually puts money into your business. Everything else takes it out. It is fundamentally important to grow this.

5. **Customer loyalty.** After you've closed the sale, it's about keeping them – for life. Make them advocates and raving fans. Customer loyalty is when people will not leave you just because something is cheaper or fancier or newer elsewhere – they truly belong to you. You should be building this because it's cheaper to keep a customer than it is to find a new one. You need to keep being relevant and valuable.

6. **Team.** Team is last because at this point you are growing with people on your team who are better than you. You are growing them for the long term. They are involved and included and as interested in the success of your business as you are. You are leading and they are following.

I've broken these pillars into three clusters. This is the structural approach to your business. It gets you thinking a little bit further than survival and just putting money in the bank today. If you can design it well before you execute, you have a much better chance of identifying problems as they arise and ultimately reaching your goals.

The first cluster – operations and finance – is part of managing the businessflow of your business. Do you have a clear understanding of the basics of finance and the numbers? How are you going to execute to achieve your goal of predictable workflow and predictable profit? How are you designing your business for the mid and long term, so that you have something to reference? Whether you are running a fish and chip shop or a $500 million company you must be on top of these aspects of your business. You must create a systemised, process-driven business. They are key considerations in how you get things done every day.

The next two – marketing and sales – are part of your lead-flow process; how you attract and secure customers. And your customer loyalty and team are related to your cashflow; how you keep your customers coming back so that the cash register keeps ringing. At some point there will need to be a team that does this just as well – if not better – than you do.

Getting these flows right is crucial to creating predictable profits in your business. They are discussed in detail in chapter 11.

Think about the Acropolis in Greece. It was built on solid foundations for the long term. It has survived wars, erosion, changes in the environment, extremes of weather. It was built for sustainability. Your business must be the same. If you do it right your business will be around a long time after you are gone, just like the Acropolis. So don't be satisfied with the same old attitude; aim to be exceptional and sustainable. These are the six fundamental pillars you must continue to grow. Know what the cut of your business is going to be and work towards it with confidence and clarity.

SERVANT TO YOUR CURRENT AND FUTURE CLIENTS

Do you aim to satisfy your customers? Is this the key to your customer service approach? Is this the culture you are creating in your business? If you answered *yes* to these questions you might think you have your customer service approach all sorted – but I'm sorry to tell you that you don't. Just *satisfying* your customers is no longer enough. It's an old-fashioned approach that says you give your customers exactly what they want and no more.

If one of my clients told me they were satisfied with my service I'd be very disappointed because it means I've missed a chance to grow my business. Each client presents you with two great opportunities: the opportunity to turn them into life-long customers and the opportunity to have them bring more customers to you because they were so impressed with your service. Just satisfying them means you met the minimum standard they expected – that's hardly going to get them excited about coming back to you next time or calling their friends and telling them about how awesome your business is. It's going to have them looking elsewhere to see if a business other than yours can do more than just meet their minimum requirements. For sustainable long-term growth you cannot be satisfied with satisfaction.

So, if this approach is not going to cut it, what should you be aiming for? You need to *delight* your customers. You need to surprise them, to exceed their expectations, to meet their every need – and then do more. We all know business is a competitive game, and if one of your competitors is out their *delighting* their customers while you're just *satisfying* them, before too long you'll be sitting in an empty store or a quiet office wondering where all of your satisfied clients went. Your business must have a *customer delight culture*.

As you shape your business for the long term it's critical that you stay humble and grounded, and that you respect the clients who are giving you the opportunity to serve them. You must aim to develop relationships of mutual benefit, and this starts with providing them with a value proposition and then following through on it. They have chosen your business and given you their money based on what you have promised to deliver to them, so meeting these expectations must be the basis of your relationships with your customers.

But, this won't necessarily keep them coming back. You keep them coming back by going *above and beyond* what you promised to deliver, by doing something unexpected that is *of value to them*. The cut of your business must include shaping it so that you never lose clients. Show them that you care and always do the right thing by them. This is vital to sustainable long-term growth because attracting customers to your business is expensive and time-consuming; once you've done that hard work, it's much more profitable to keep these people in your stable rather than let them leave and then have to find new customers who want to buy from you. Repeat customers and referrals provide a much higher ROI for your business.

It's not hard to figure out if you are good at this or not. Clients who have already handed their money over to you and experienced your products and service are a barometer for your customer service systems; if they keep coming back you are clearly on the right track. If they buy from you once and you never see them again, clearly this side of your business needs work. People want to – and sometimes are *desperate* to – find businesses they can deal with on a regular basis. A good mechanic or electrician or physiotherapist or accountant is worth their weight in gold. When you have a problem you want fixed you don't want the added hassle of having to find somebody who can help you or dealing with a person you don't know. You want to be able to jump on the phone and call up your regular guy or girl because you *know* they will give you what you need. They will get you from A to B. In your customers' eyes you need to be the number 1 option. In fact, you need to be the *only* option.

You can develop systems that will help you delight your customers and keep them coming back. These are called **Retention Strategies,** and they are an important part of growing your business. Not having these systems in place means you have an **I'm Going to Keep Finding New Clients Every Week Because I Don't look after my Existing Clients Properly and Soon I'm Going to go Broke** strategy. We look at Retention Strategies in detail in the next section because they are part of the colour of your business, so keep reading!

Think about how powerful word of mouth is. We all tell friends, family and business associates about our experiences with other businesses, good and bad. What will people be saying about *your* business?

IGAs

If you think an IGA is just a supermarket you are missing out on opportunities to grow, because when it comes to your business an IGA is an **Income Growth Activity**. These are activities that you can do *every day* to actively increase the income of your business.

We've already looked at some of these. It's an extension of the tools and concepts discussed so far; for example, adding a zero to your hourly rate. We load these activities into the default diary as IGAs. That's where you get your discipline and follow-through. As part of the cut of your business, you should start doing five IGAs every day. That's five things every day that actively help you generate income. Some of these are simple and will only take a few minutes. For example, call or email three potential new clients. Have lunch with an existing client and see what else you can do for them. Look at your diary and get rid of one thing that you really don't need to be doing. Study the systems in your business and see where improvements can be made. There's an endless number of small and large things that will increase the income of your business over the long term. Don't confuse *activity* with *productivity*; make sure you are spending time doing things that will add dollars to your bottom line. Be committed and focused and follow through on the productive activities that really count.

Schedule in your diary the IGAs you need to be doing every day, every week and every month. Spend some time on long-term plans such as building strategic partnerships or developing new products that you know your clients want. This might not put money in the bank next week but it will in a year or two. A good strategic partnership can bring hundreds of A-grade clients to your business over the next few years. Also spend time on short-term strategies such as getting feedback from clients, or giving a talk at the business association, or running a targeted marketing campaign. I usually suggest people spend around 70% of their IGA time on short-term activities and 30% on long-term activities, but you can vary this to suit yourself and your business. Always keep in mind how quickly long-term becomes short-term. Have a think about how decisions you made 12 months ago are affecting you now. It seemed a long way off at the time, but here you are, right now, living with the results of those decisions it now seems like you made just yesterday. As the leader of your business it's your job to be looking ahead and seeing the problems before they arrive, so that you can avoid them if possible and be equipped to deal with them if not.

EXERCISE: 10 IGAs

Write down 10 IGAs that you could schedule into your diary:

1. ____

2. ____

3. ____

4. ____

5. ____

6. ____

7. ____

8. ____

9. ____

10. ____

PLAY DUMB AND DIG DEEP

People often look a bit confused when I tell them to play dumb and dig deep – and that's probably fair enough! So let me explain…

Playing dumb with your clients means having a culture of curiosity. It's about listening to your clients – *really* listening – and developing a deep and genuine understanding of what they want and need from you. Most people who start a business do so because they are an expert in their particular field, and this can serve them very well. But it's important to be fully aware that you don't have all the answers, and that to delight your customers you need to listen to them, not be arrogant and egotistical and *tell* them what they need. Play dumb and learn from your clients. They have a lot to teach you.

Digging deep is about getting to the bottom of what your customers really desire. Spend as much time as needed with them until you are confident you have really reached the core of why they came to you and what they want. You need to be exhaustive in asking questions before you start providing answers. You need to use your expertise and experience to serve your customers well, not to make assumptions about what they need. Don't be afraid to ask your clients as many questions as you need to. This doesn't make you look like you don't know what you're doing, it shows the customer you are truly interested in what their frustration is and how you can best solve it for them. Ask breakthrough questions that will truly get you to the bottom of the problem.

I heard this story from a friend of mine recently. His mum needed a new computer because her old one had started to run slowly, so she went into the local computer store and told the young man her problem. Being a computer geek, he heard only two words – 'it's slow' – so he sold her the fastest warp-speed computer he had. He told her it would 'future proof' her and featured the new Mega-gizmo 7.0 and a graphics this and a wireless that and be compatible with blah blah blah, and all of it was *faaaaaaaaast*. But there's *faaaaaaaaast* and then there's just fast. My friend's mum only needed fast. She only used email and would 'look at Google' – as such she had been sold a machine that was completely in excess of her needs. When my friend saw the new computer he told his mum she'd paid way too much for a whole lot of things she didn't need. Do you think she was a delighted customer?

This computer salesman didn't play dumb and he didn't dig deep. He was only interested in a one-off sale not a long-term customer. Because he knew computers and she didn't, he thought it was his job to tell her what she needed; instead, a five-minute chat about how she used her computer would have seen him direct her to the right one. He wouldn't have made as much on this sale because he didn't sell her the top end model, *but* he would have had a delighted customer who would have come back to him every few years when she needed a new computer because she trusted him to sell her what she needed, and this is worth much more to the business over the long term. *That's* how you build a sustainable business.

The other thing lost with this poor approach is the potential for a referral, and this could have happened the next day. So not only does this salesman lose the potential for a long-term client, the short-term opportunity cost in missed referrals can be huge.

Are you building for future growth by playing dumb and digging deep? Do you have a culture of curiosity? Do you listen to your customers or just sell them what suits you?

Having the best products in the world won't help you if you don't connect with your clients. It's about win–win outcomes; they get the service they need – and more – so they are happy, and you've created a customer for life, so you're happy.

Remember: **Get brilliant at the basics.**

 ## CHAPTER GEMS

- The Quality of Life Ladder gives you a process that will lead to great results for your business and a high quality of life for you.
- The Six Pillars to Exceptional Growth are the foundations for the success of your business.
- Get brilliant at the basics.
- You need to delight your customers, not just satisfy them.
- IGAs are activities that you can do every day to actively increase the income of your business.

CASE STUDY: The Cartridge Family

The Cartridge Family (TCF) is a family-run printer and consumables supply business that supplies businesses across Australia and New Zealand. Currently the happy husband and wife team employ five wonderful staff who ship stock from their warehouse in Melbourne or from third-party warehouses across both countries.

The industry is massive – everyone prints – and comprises three sectors:

- large and corporate;
- SME; and
- home business (or home-consumer) printing.

TCF supplies millions of dollars of genuine cartridges and printers to the SME market plus a small number of large corporate businesses. They are also preferred suppliers to a small number of buying groups, associations and not-for-profit organisations.

However, running a family business presents a number of problems, such as communication, delineation of roles and responsibilities and keeping focused. This is why they sought help. Here is how they answered the following questions.

1. At what point did you recognise that you needed help, and what motivated you to get it?

Danielle always knew she was better motivated by others and wanted a coach. The typical nature of the sales and marketer works better with targets and accountability. David is a self-motivated finance and admin specialist who didn't (and doesn't) enjoy being externally motivated. The key was finding the right coach and mentor that we could both work with.

2. What did you learn that helped you solve these problems?

Initially, simply understanding critical numbers and the importance of knowing them as a sales and marketer had a massive influence over the way that Danielle performed her duties and reported on the state of the customer list that she was responsible for. This clarity meant that a way forward could clearly be identified and tracked.

Having a space to talk about the 'family business' and communication issues meant that not every discussion ended in a communication breakdown.

3. What systems have you put in place that have helped your business?

TCF has implemented four customer delight systems that have resulted in many years' loyalty from our customers.

- **Transactional delight system, a small sweet** – the lolly frog – that is shipped with every order or invoice, depending on which comes from the office first.

- **An annual delight system** – our non-branded birthday gift – that goes to the top 800 or so customers every year on their birthday. The item, which is changed at the start of each financial year, is engraved or embroidered with the customer's name.

- **A random delight system** – a range of small gifts that can be despatched for any reason.

- **A 'sorry' system.** TCF staff have a small budget to apologise properly in the event of mistakes, either TCF mistakes, courier mistakes or supplier mistakes. Of course the problem is fixed first.

Putting systems into place with relation to staffing was also implemented. Regular team meetings contribute to better communication and better results for the customer experience.

4. What was the biggest single change you made to yourself or your business that helped turn things around?

Employing staff. But prior to employing staff, Danielle had to learn to be accountable to the tasks that needed to be undertaken so that the business could afford staff. David needed to take the chance that staff would help and not burn us. Our previous foray into staffing was expensive with no results. The very first thing that our coach helped us to do was fire that staff member.

5. What other changes have you made and how have they helped?

Many things contribute to the success of a business. At its core, the development of the leaders of the business, in self-confidence, in self-belief and in knowing their 'WHY?' means that leaders can make positive changes and take a chance on trying new things and growing.

Discovering her 'WHY?' meant that Danielle has a compelling reason to do the work that she had committed to in the business.

With the growth in self-understanding, Danielle was able to achieve positive sales outcomes. Her networking improved and sales results grew as well. Marketing efforts became more targeted and financially viable. One of the successful strategies that made a big impact on the business was sponsoring and exhibiting to meet new customers. The accountability to follow up yielded strong success.

Moving out of the home office after 12 years also grew the business. In the years following, TCF staff grew from two to five. Vendors such as HP and Brother saw greater potential in TCF as a result of this more professional space and gave TCF better opportunities. Some of those opportunities ended up in national media coverage and external investment in other, online opportunities.

6. What fears or challenges did you have to overcome? How did you do this?

Certainly the challenge of liking each other as a husband and wife team as well as business partners was tenuous before we employed our coach. Today our relationship has not only weathered those storms but grown massively. Today we hold a role model status to other families in business and share some of the ways we did so.

One way was to become and remain separate in our responsibilities in the business. Certainly where the roles of finance/admin cross over with sales/marketing (such as in budgeting and reporting) there needs to be interest and collaboration. We honed that ability to not get involved with each other's areas unless invited or unless budgeting and reporting became an issue.

7. What advice do you have for other small business owners who are currently struggling?

Get a coach, get a coach, get a coach. But make sure it is the right coach. So much money can be wasted with the wrong coach or coaching system. Interviewing a number of coaches with the benefits of knowing their weaknesses and threats will mean that you can easily find the right coach to fit both your budget and expectations. Having clarity around the results or targets you want to meet before the engagement of a coach will also mean that the arrangement can be targeted and tracked to the benefit of all. No coach wants to work with clients who are not set to succeed.

8. How is your business performing now? Has this exceeded your expectations?

Business is flying. David and Danielle are travelling the world and the staff are delighted to be part of their team.

9. What specific goals in dollar terms have you achieved from implementing the changes you have made?

Gaining and maintaining the multimillion dollar status of the business was important.

10. What specific non-monetary goals have you achieved?

Self-development, self-confidence, and the ability now to step out and grow Danielle's personal brands has been a positive move.

11. What changes do you still need to make to your business and why?

Better staff communication can always benefit our business. A better and more comprehensive marketing plan is currently called for and better time management will help too.

12. Where do you think your business will be in five years' time?

We have never wanted to grow to a $20 million business. We do not believe that TCF can maintain its excellence in the industry with too many staff, or too many customers. Certainly the growth of a couple of major customers will alleviate any stress of losing other major customers.

If, in five years' time TCF is where it is today, with a strong plan for the exit strategy where our children run the business, we will be happy.

13. If you hadn't made an effort to get help, where do you think you would be right now?

No idea, it doesn't warrant focusing on. 17 years into our marriage may not have been a reality though.

14. What are your top five tips for other business owners?

1. Get coached.
2. As leaders in your business, develop easy-to-implement systems that frontline staff can implement and consistently follow through with.
3. Always follow up with your leads and connections.
4. Network more effectively.
5. Develop your self-confidence and your self-belief – with clarity and with purpose.

15. What big goal have you recently achieved in your business?

We've signed on another New Zealand buying group.

16. What big goal have you recently achieved in your life?

We've travelled extensively, and have an upcoming Mediterranean Cruise.

Part 3: Colour

" Business is a game, played for fantastic stakes, and you're in competition with experts. If you want to win, you have to learn to be a master of the game. "

—Sidney Sheldon, 'Master of the Game'

The colour of your business is about the internal processes that create predictability for profitability. Profitability by itself is no good without predictability. I've met business owners who make $100,000 profit one month and $10,000 the next. The boom months are exciting but the troughs are a disaster, and they have no systems in place to tell them what is coming around the corner or what the next month is going to bring, and no plans to smooth it out. Businesses that operate like this are always only three feet away from disaster, and they'll never see it coming. So burn this into your brain right now – predictability is just as important as profitability. When I look at my own business I can tell you with clarity and confidence how much profit we'll be making in the coming months and exactly how and why we'll be making it. You need this level of predictability to be able to make good decisions about where your business is going, otherwise you are just hoping and guessing.

We're now getting into some deep stuff. Colour is where you can really start to move and shake. This is where you begin to change your environment and what is going on around you. This is the game. It's time to think carefully about how you deal with clients, who you associate with at work and away from it, and the physical aspects of your workplace.

Excited? I am! So let's get into it!

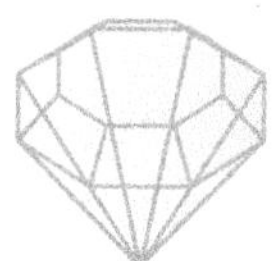

10. UNLEASHING THE POWER OF YOUR CUSTOMERS

CREATING A CUSTOMER DELIGHT CULTURE

As you know by now a key part of the colour of your business is how you treat your customers. This is an aspect of business that I love. I get pumped about this every day. Doing things with your customers that are above and beyond is a very cool thing to do.

In the section on cut we discussed the need for a Customer Delight Culture in your business. It's hugely important. Without customers your business is nothing, even if you have the greatest products or services in the world. If people aren't buying, you have an expensive hobby not a business.

So let's have a look at how you delight your customers. Not satisfy, *delight*.

If you want your customers to come back to you time and time and time again, just meeting their needs is not good enough. There are dozens, and maybe even hundreds, of other businesses out there that will meet your customers' needs just as well as you can. It's the minimum standard to be in business at all. To build a prosperous and sustainable machine that puts money in your pocket for years to come, you need to be proactive and think outside the square when it comes to dealing with customers.

You need to keep getting better and be an innovator. You can't simply wait until there's a problem and then step in and help. You need to offer the solution to the problem, *and more*. You need to see the problem before they do. You should always be communicating with your customers and seeing what else you can do to help – there will always be something. If you run a gym, can you open up a small crèche to look after the kids while the parents do a workout? If you're a mechanic, start washing your customers' cars at no extra cost. If you sell computers, throw in a free game with every computer sold so the kids can't wait to get home and use it. Go above and beyond. That's how you delight your customers. That's how you keep them coming back.

If you own a restaurant, feed them! Have an abundance mindset, don't have an attitude of scarcity. Give them an extra glass of wine. Keep bringing them bread throughout the meal. Bring a free bowl of chips for the kids. The small cost will disappear into insignificance when you start turning your customers into raving fans who come back to your restaurant time and time again and they also tell their friends.

Make a Customer Delight Culture a non-negotiable part of the colour of your business. Don't just serve your customers, wow them! Make sure all your staff have the same approach. Show them that you care, not with a fake smile and a voucher for $10 off next time but by *genuinely* caring and being interested. Play dumb and dig deep. Make them feel as if they are the most important customer you have ever served – because they are. Each and every client is vital to the ongoing success of your business.

A great question to ask yourself is, 'How can I give my customers something more than they expect?' It's simple but powerful. And here's the key to creating a true Customer Delight Culture: you need to think outside the box when you answer this question. A crèche in a gym, washing cars for a mechanic and free games with a computer are great steps in the right direction, but they are just the beginning. What about giving your clients movie tickets, or a voucher for a restaurant, or sending flowers on their birthday? Business owners often look a bit surprised when I make these suggestions. It usually goes something like this: 'But I run a *gym*; why would I give them *movie tickets*?' I want you to have a think about this right now. Why *would* you give them movie tickets? Do you have the answer yet? Think about it... It's actually really simply. You'd give them movie tickets *because they'll love it!* That's it! It doesn't necessarily need to be related to your business. It doesn't always have to be something they'll expect from you or related to your products or services. Imagine if you signed up for a gym membership and you received a welcome letter that contained two gold class movie tickets. Or you picked your car up from the mechanic and the tickets were sitting on the front seat. Wouldn't you be blown away? Wouldn't you tell your friends? I sure would.

A fantastic example of a company that has created a customer delight culture is The Cartridge Family. Have a look back at the previous case study and their customer delight system that has "resulted in many years' loyalty" from their customers.

THE CRITICAL NON-ESSENTIALS MATRIX

What are five things *you* can do for *your* customers that are critical for them to be delighted but that are not essential? Let's have a look at what I call the **Critical Non-essentials Matrix** (CNE).

Below are five random and surprising examples of what you can do to delight your clients. The key is the surprise element. If it's not surprising it will become an essential and lose its impact. If your client expects something it won't wow them nearly as much. So:

* Give them a hand-written thank you card thanking them for their custom and achievement.
* Buy them movie tickets. And don't be cheap – get gold-class tickets.
* Give them a free product or service upgrade or a voucher for a related business.
* Take them out for a coffee, or lunch or dinner.
* Send them a gift on their birthday (not a voucher for your business – this is not an opportunity to get another sale, it's an opportunity to wow your customer).

Now let's have a look at how each of these fits into the Critical Non-essentials Matrix. If you have a look at the diagram opposite you'll see that we have 'cost' going from low to high on the vertical axis and 'level of difficulty' going from easy to hard on the horizontal axis. What you have to do now is fit each of these five bonuses for your customers into the matrix according to cost and degree of difficulty. You can see I've done it for the five examples.

The CNE Matrix

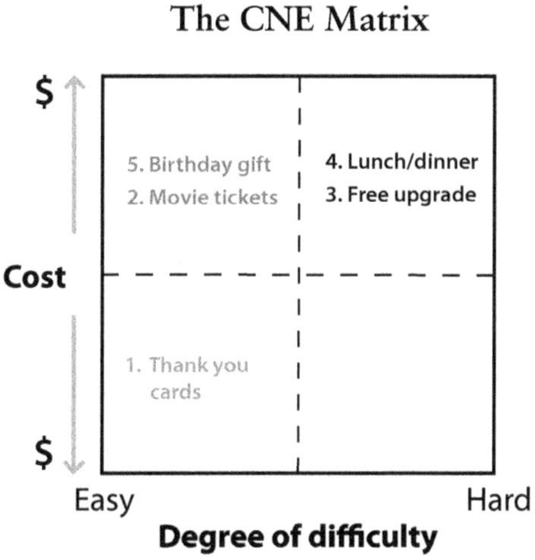

EXERCISE: Critical non-essentials

Prepare a list like this for your business. You can use these five, or you can come up with five other bonuses that you think will be more appropriate for your customers. It's also a good idea to work out a timeframe over which these events occur, so as part of your plan you need to work out what actions you are going to take over a period of – for example – six months. Then, draw yourself a diagram like the one above, and insert each of these items in the appropriate place.

This matrix allows you to decide how you will use these five activities in your business. Thank you cards are of course cheap and easy. Movie tickets and a gift will probably cost a bit more but are also easy. A meal with a client takes a bit more effort, as does an upgrade.

Your low cost and easy ideas must be done often. There's no excuse not to do them. The more expensive and difficult things are done when appropriate, but they must still be done. Don't think of these as a cost, think of them as an investment in the long-term success of your business. And once you have this system and culture in place, don't think that you need to stop at five – keep going! Keep coming up with new and inventive ways to delight your current and future customers.

Let's have a look at how it works. Let's say you own and manage a gym. Your system for delighting your customers might go something like this:

* When they sign up with you, you send a hand-written thank you note and a free extra month on their membership.
* You send them a voucher for a sports store on their birthday (you know the date because it's on the membership form).
* After they've been with you for one year you send them a couple of gold class movie tickets to congratulate them on their commitment to their health and fitness.
* On their birthday in their second year of membership you give them a free membership upgrade.
* At the completion of their second year of membership you invite them and a friend into the gym for a free personal training session with you.

How does that sound? Would you ever lose a customer? Not likely. Would they talk about your gym at a dinner party on Friday night, and tell all their friends they should sign up? You bet they would.

It is essential to have systems in place in your business to manage your customer interactions. We refer to this as client fulfilment. It's also essential to have a staff member accountable for this who will ensure you have customers coming back time and time again. If you don't have somebody in place to lead and manage this process it will only happen when people get around to it, and that's not good enough.

Caring about your clients is non-negotiable. Do whatever it takes to wow them and show them that you care. Play the game as if you are a global leader and eventually you will be. Your customers will always expect you to get better over time, so don't let them down. Whatever you did last year, do more this year. Do it bigger and better. *Delight* them.

UNLEASHING THE TRUE POWER OF YOUR CUSTOMERS

One of the greatest challenges we face in the world today is the speed with which things get done and the lack of time to genuinely care or even do them right. Relationships are made at lightning speed, often leading to win/lose results. In the world of business, customers are getting angry and complaining; service-providers are getting frustrated to the point that they are resenting and walking away from their businesses. Countless small businesses promise something to their customers and then fail to deliver. We've all been there. The cause: a less than aligned team culture and inferior training that compromises employees' good intentions. Too many business owners and teams are drawn to the quick fix and the cheaper option. They are focused on closing the sale that's in front of them, not on building a long-term relationship with a client. The lack of long-term strategy is creating long-term growth issues. Everyone is in a hurry for success and recognition. The problem is that we are not committing the time and energy to the fundamentals that ensure we are unleashing the power of our A-grade customers. The result is that over 90% of small businesses are facing a customer loyalty crisis.

So how do we unleash the power of our customers? To start with, we have to embrace ownership of the challenge and not take the position of denial that they are simply an annoyance that has to be dealt with. I'm always stunned when I hear business owners complain about having to deal with customers. If you see customers as a hassle, don't worry – very soon you won't have any left and you won't have to deal with them any more. Won't that be great!

To unlock the vault to long-term profits you need to view customers as being your principal partners in success – because that's exactly what they are. Stop asking *why* ('Why aren't they doing what we want?') and start asking *how* ('How can we provide what they need?').

There are four customers in every business and you need to care about all of them. The owner is the primary customer. Second, are the employees. Third, are suppliers. And finally, the most important customer is the customer themselves – the person or organisation that is buying your product or service. Most valuable are those who buy from you repeatedly and bring many more customers to you. As long as you keep on delivering just a little more than you promised every time, this is what will happen. The key is to consistently 'under promise and over deliver', and you do this with the right systems in place and a Customer Delight

Culture. This is the foundation of your business growth. Without customers there is no business – it's just you running around with a business card playing make-believe.

The Complete Customer Suite

Customers

Owner

Business customers

Suppliers

Team

Building a reputation based on service is crucial to your long-term profitability. It's a critical differentiation. You must ensure that there is ongoing investment in training and education around your value proposition for you and your team.

Then you need an understanding of the key metrics to building a raving fan base. It starts with the mantra of being aligned and non-negotiable for unleashing the power of your customer community or 'tribe'.

It is also vital to build a small business that learns to say *no* to its non-desired market. You must be valued by and attractive to the target market you serve. You can only truly unleash the power of your customers once you get out of the way of your business. This means playing the game with an attitude of abundance, not scarcity. Your aim should be to build a business where 80% of your customers are ideal and contribute directly to your profits. You want to be there for them today, next year and in 10 years time. Spending time with non-ideal clients is a huge opportunity cost – you could be spending your time much more profitably. People who are not in your target market are unlikely to become repeat customers, so think carefully about how – or if – you serve them.

In my experience over the last 20-plus years in building small businesses for myself and as a globally acclaimed business coach, I have come to understand the power of investing in ideal customers – the ones your business deserves. Embrace the culture of doing whatever it takes to keep them for life. This is the real ethos of customer service, taking action to create value for someone else with a big smile. This leads to loyalty, which leads to repeat business. Even more valuable than that is referral business, which is at the heart of the most profitable businesses in the world today.

RESULTS + RETENTION = REFERRALS WHICH EQUALS PROFIT × 2

You need to consistently provide the results for which people have backed you. You need to deliver the promised result on time and on budget. It's not about your products or services but the overall outcome you provide for your clients. Getting results for your customers and clients is about doing the right thing. It's about meeting – and then exceeding – their expectations. If you do this you will keep them for life – they won't need to go anywhere else.

And if you do this, not only will you retain your existing customers, you will attract new ones. Chances are your delighted customers are going to talk to others who are looking for the same solution. They'll happily recommend you. Referrals come from people who were on their way to a bridge when you stepped in and guided them across yours. Once you've taken them from A to B and they are delighted on the other side, then *they* will help guide people across your bridge for you! It's almost like an unpaid sales team. And even better, we all trust referrals when they come from somebody we know, so we're much more likely to act on them. It's an unpaid and highly trustworthy sales team! Can you think of *anything* better for your business?

When your business runs like this, two people profit from every transaction. Your client is happy because you have taken them from frustration to freedom, and you are happy because your delighted customer will come back again and again and also refer others to your business. This is the greatest business model anywhere, ever. It looks like this:

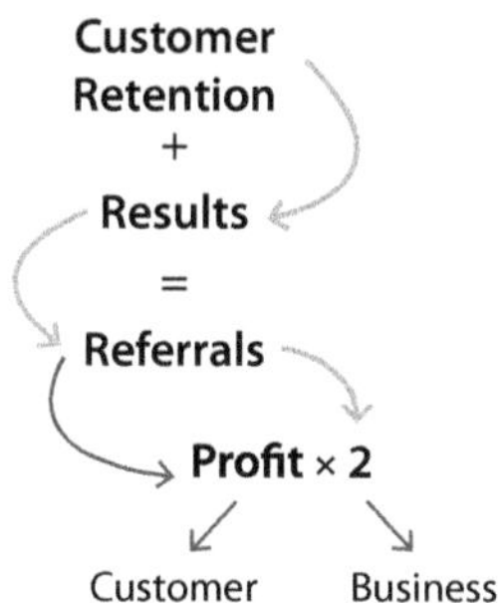

There is a distinct difference between loyalty and repeat business. Loyalty is much more valuable. Loyalty is when your customers are not swayed by cheaper, trendy or newer products. They continue doing business with you as they trust that your innovation will continuously be improved.

Loyal customers don't bother researching the competition or entertaining other options. Loyalty is not easily won, hence it takes a very committed business to build a 'customer community' that is genuinely for life. I have a friend who *always* goes to the same store when he needs new electronic gadgets. He doesn't even look anywhere else. I asked him why, and he said he has tried many different stores over the years but he had always found the best service at this particular store, so now he doesn't even bother to shop around. How's that for customer loyalty? That's what you need to be aiming for.

To help you discover how you can build this in your business, as an exercise I strongly suggest you pick up the phone and contact 10 of your best and 10 of your perceived challenging customers and ask them to give you some brutal truth about your business and how you interact with them – don't be scared, it may not be that bad! It may not be that good either. What's critical is how you respond.

Address the concerns of your most valued customers. Then do an exercise in 'community' identification. Determine which customers you are currently serving who you wish to de-select and say 'thanks but no thanks' to. Don't act on emotion. Be brave and confirm with clarity and logic which customers you will be pruning from your customer base. Make this decision based on who you want as part of your future global business. Remember to include all four relevant customers in your research.

Be honest about communicating with your clients to help build your business as you provide them with the results they want. Ask them what you do well, what you could do better, why they came to you – anything that will help you serve them better in the future. It is a good and very reasonable conversation to be having. Many business owners don't do this because they feel they are imposing, but it's not imposing at all. It's asking them to help, and in return they'll get bigger and better service from you. If you turn your customers into raving fans they will be more than happy to have this conversation with you.

Success is not an event, it's a process and a mindset. In world-class businesses it's an ongoing process of change and evolution. Creating a big smile for your clients can only lead to results and retention, and to keep them smiling you need to keep getting better at what you do and increasing what you are offering them. If you are not going forward you are going backwards. There is no in between. Providing great service is an investment in your business that creates an ongoing cycle of further growth and provides increasing ROI for your clients. Here's a simple formula that shows the benefits of continually increasing your service to your clients:

> **Increasing service**
> = increasing ROI for clients
> = increasing A-grade clients
> = increasing ROI for both your clients and your business.

Everybody wins! And a cycle is created whereby the investment you make today provides a boost to your profits in the future, which allows you to then make further investments in your service, which provides further growth, and on and on it goes…It looks like this:

↑ **Service**

=

↑ **Feeling better** (emotional connections – ESP)

=

↑ **A-grade clients** (community – CSP)

=

↑ **Profit**

The reality is that four out of five small businesses don't make it over five years. Globally, less than 7% reach over $2 million in turnover in one year. The critical skills and tools that are required to create an idea are very different to the critical skills and tools needed to grow a business. The miracle is in growing the business. Having the right customers and treating them well is crucial to your survival and growth.

Business is an intellectual sport. It requires a scoreboard that is brutally honest and a culture that strives for excellence and personal best. Both of these are moving targets. Once executed with consistency there is always a new level to strive for. If you want to be in the top 10% in your industry – not the 90% that are falling behind – discover and unleash the power of your A-grade customers.

 ## CHAPTER GEMS

- Doing things with your customers that are above and beyond is a very cool thing to do.
- What are five things you can do for your customers that are critical for them to be delighted but not essential?
- To unlock the vault to long-term profits you need to view customers as being your principal partners in success.
- Results + Retention = Referrals which equals profit × 2

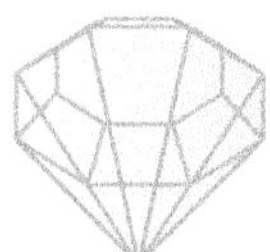

11. MAKING THE PROFITS FLOW

HOW LEADFLOW TURNS INTO DREAMFLOW

Once you've designed your business it's time to get down to the day-to-day running of things. Even while you are making day-to-day decisions you must continue to stay focused on the longer term rather than worrying that 'I didn't make a sale today'.

Your sales and marketing structure – two of your six pillars – is what starts the miracle that will end up with you achieving your dreams. Sounds unlikely? Take a look at the diagram overleaf.

We're all in business for ourselves because we want to achieve our dreams. Ultimately there is no other reason. Your dreams are at the end of a long process that starts with how many leads you generate for your business.

Leadflow to Dreamflow

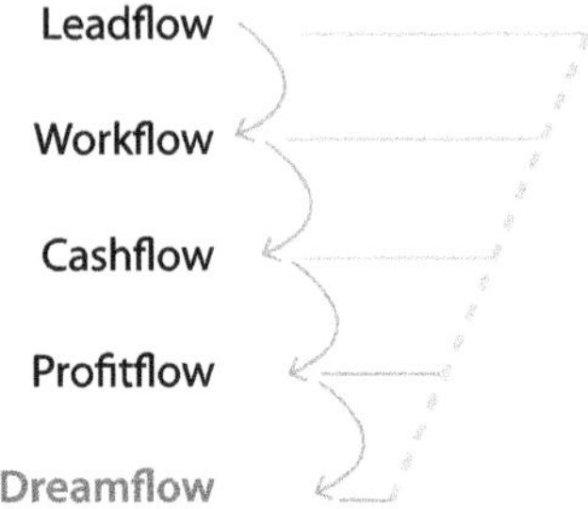

Let's work backwards to understand this process.

What do you need to make your dreams come true? Steady, predictable profitflows over the long term.

What do you need to generate profitflows over the long term? Steady, predictable cashflow.

Where does cashflow come from? A steady flow of business that's delivered on time and on budget by a team that's focused on structure and predictability.

And a steady flow of leads – combined with a good sales structure – is needed to generate work. If you don't have leads on potential clients in your target market you'll just sit around all day surfing the internet because you have nobody to sell to. So, a good leadflow leads to a continuous stream of work in the business and ultimately to your dreams.

Profitflow only occurs when there's a consistency to cashflow. Having a great month or a great quarter is just not good enough. It won't get you to your dreams.

Many businesses that think they have a cashflow problem really don't. They actually have a *leadflow* problem. If you don't have enough potential clients in the desired target market moving accordingly in the pipeline you have no hope of achieving the cashflow you need. And if you don't get consistent profitflow you won't reach the holy grail of dreamflow.

There is one other way to reach your dreams, and that is to go into debt. But this is only a short-term option and won't deliver you a dreamflow. You might be able to go on that one trip or buy that nice car, but that will be it. Far from achieving all your goals, you'll achieve the first one and then be stuck paying it off for the next 20 years. I don't think that's what most people dream of.

So don't get ahead of yourself and get into enormous debt. That's a short-term plan with a huge downside. Wait until your business is consistently producing the profits you need to fulfil *all* of your dreams. It's far better to wait an extra few years and do it properly than to get greedy and want everything now. So many bad decisions are made when the focus is short term rather than long term. Think about where you could be now if you'd made better long-term decisions five years ago.

The quality of your decision-making is pivotal. There's no such thing as a bad business, only bad decisions. It all started with a great idea. You know that. You wouldn't have put in the time and money and effort if you thought it was a bad idea, so that means your business is struggling because you've made some bad decisions. And that's okay, because that means you can do something about it.

It starts with leadflow, having a continuous 24/7 approach to attracting and engaging A-grade clients, and ultimately making it easier for them to buy from you. This will in turn build up your work in progress. (Workflow is *work in progress* flow.) Continual growth and delivery of work in progress leads to continual cashflow, which leads to continuous profitflow, which leads to continuous dreamflow.

FLOW AND THE SIX PILLARS TO EXCEPTIONAL GROWTH

Right now you're probably thinking, *that's all well and good, but how do I do that? What steps do I take in my business to make this all happen?* This is where we return to the Six Pillars to Exceptional Growth, because each of those pillars relates to the flows of your business.

Businessflow

The initial pillars of **operations** and **finance** influence the processes and scoreboard of your business. You need to have designed your business and how you intend for it to function predictably for profits. You also need to ensure that the business has relevant scoreboards for your reflection and your understanding of its strategic progress. To maximise businessflow you need to constantly review your systems and results, and be familiar with your business plan every 90 days.

Tips for creating a strong businessflow for predictable profits:
- undertake five income-generating activities (IGAs) every day
- achieve a fair return for your daily exertion
- have a financial plan in place, and stick to it
- have a formula to double – and then triple – your profits
- test and measure *everything*
- use a default diary
- constantly reflect and improve on your performance.

Leadflow

The pillars of **marketing** and **sales** influence the work in progress of your business. As I have said, it's all about attracting future A-grade clients and making it easy for them to buy from you. It's about finding the right people *and* having systems in place that ensure they buy from you. You must understand the profile of your desired target market, understand how much each lead costs you, and have a successful sales funnel in place.

Tips for creating a strong leadflow for attracting A-grade customers and making it easy for them to buy from you:

- have referral systems in place
- set your website up to capture leads
- develop strategic relationships that refer clients to your business
- reactivate past clients
- have extreme follow-up systems
- measure and understand your conversion rates
- have a well-planned marketing budget that you are committed to.

Cashflow

The pillars of **customer loyalty** and **team** influence the cashflow of your business. There is immense cash-pulling power in a repeat-based and referral-based business run by a champion team.

Tips for creating a strong cashflow for repeat business referrals and keeping customers for life:

- create a customer delight culture
- be in constant communication with your customers

- know the lifetime value of your customers as a dollar amount and treat them accordingly
- have staff who understand their roles and are well trained for them
- have team meetings every week that are effective and action-oriented
- build a team-culture based around tenacity and an attitude of 'whatever it takes'.

THE TEN DREAMFLOW COMMANDMENTS

Leadflow, businessflow and cashflow are the life-blood of any business. You need a steady flow of leads coming into your business to generate the work that gets delivered on time and on budget that turns into steady cashflow so that you can meet your financial commitments as they arise and ultimately have enough money in the bank to achieve your dreams.

Here are **The Ten Dreamflow Commandments** that will ensure your business is always ahead of the game and always has enough money in the bank to pay the bills and ensure the owner is also being rewarded:

1. **Thou shalt be persistent.** You have to be proactive. You have to. You can't sit back in your office and wait for the clients to come knocking, because they won't. You have to go out and find them and then do whatever it takes to get them through your door. You must go slow to go fast, be committed, and proceed with confidence and clarity. Stay on track and stick to your plan.

2. **Thou shalt be resilient.** We all know business can be tough. Are you going to let problems get in your way and keep you from your dreams? Or are you going to do what it takes to get yourself back on track?

3. **Thou shalt have tenacity.** I can coach all the other commandments but this is your responsibility. I can't coach this. You have to be tenacious about 1% improvements every day. It is your hand on that dial. Personal best is the game.

4. **Thou shalt proceed with velocity.** Get it done today. Get it done right now. Don't leave what needs to be done today until tomorrow.

5. **Thou shalt have momentum.** If you can make five phone calls today, what would it look like if you made 20? Or 100?

6. **Thou shalt have synergy.** You need to have synergy with everybody you deal with; your staff, your clients, your suppliers. From top to bottom everybody in your organisation needs to be on the same page and moving in the same direction.

7. **Thou shalt study the scoreboard.** By now you are well aware that your finances are the scoreboard for your business. And if you don't understand the scoreboard, how do you know if you are winning or losing? You might be behind by 10 points or ahead by 50, but you won't know.

8. **Thou shalt practise brutal truth.** You can't be lazy and rich. It just can't be done. You have to make a real and honest commitment to look at yourself and your business and see what needs to be done, and then do it.

9. **Thou shalt practise congruency.** What you say and what you do are totally aligned. Your dreams should always be congruent with your current cashflow and profitflow. Don't plan for the Porsche until the required profitflow is showing up. Don't plan that trip to Disneyland until you have enough reliable profitflow.

10. **Thou shalt be humble yet assertive.** No doubt you are good at what you do but you don't know everything. Being humble yet assertive means that you take the time to listen and learn from others, but when the time comes to make a decision about your business you do so with clarity and confidence. Nobody knows your business like you do; it's your responsibility to lead it in the right direction, nobody else's.

I've been in business a long time, and I know that one of the biggest worries that keeps business owners up at night is cashflow. The Ten Dreamflow Commandments will ensure you keep your business moving in the right direction, that you stay on top of things, and that you always have enough cash coming in. If you can't create the activity required to generate work, you won't get to cashflow and you won't get to dreamflow.

Measurement and predictability

Understanding your figures is key. If it moves and shakes it needs to be measured. What doesn't get measured cannot be managed. If you show me your activities I can predict with clarity and precision your results. I once had a client who was just about out of cash and he was just days away from chucking it all in. He came to me as a last effort to salvage his struggling business. After a few months with me I could see that things were starting to turn around, but he wasn't convinced as the results weren't showing up in his bank account yet. He rang me up one day and said, "That's it. I'm done. I can't pay you anymore and I'm basically out of cash. I have to pull the plug."

I spoke to him for a long time and he filled me in on exactly what his situation was. At the end of the conversation I made him an offer. I told him that I would keep working with him as before and I'd keep invoicing him but he didn't have to pay me for 60 days. I spelled out exactly what he needed to do, and that I had absolute confidence this would right his ship within 60 days. He took some persuading but he agreed to the deal.

I got one of the best phone calls I've ever had 62 days later. He rang me up more excited than I'd ever heard him: he'd just landed a $280,000 contract for his business, the largest by a long way that he had ever secured! That was a few years ago and today his business is going from strength to strength.

It's not about the result, it's about the activity. I knew with confidence that he was only a couple of months away because of the activity of the previous 90 days. His pipeline had never been bigger. His follow-up systems had never been better. This was a result of a six-month process; he just couldn't see how it was all about to come to fruition. All the indicators – such as conversion rates and the tested and measured data – allowed me to see this. I'm not psychic, I just read the data, and you can too. I learned how to do this and you can too.

When you think you are three feet from disaster you may in fact be three feet from gold, so keep going. Just go for it. If you do all this the cashflow turns up.

MAKE REJECTION YOUR BEST FRIEND

Nobody likes rejection, right? Wrong! Rejection is my best friend, because it means I have a lead. Learn to see a 'no' as a 'not yet'. It's a challenge to get this potential customer over the line. It's not about giving them a hard sell or being a nuisance, it's about staying in touch and building a relationship and finding ways you can get them to cross your bridge.

A client I have worked with was trying to develop relationships with A-grade clients, but he was constantly rejected because of the size of his business, what was thought to be a lack of processes, and the type of clients he had worked with in the past. However, through very deliberate coaching he stayed true to his goals and he kept in touch with these potential clients. Eventually an opportunity came up when a previous supplier let the organisation down. My client was called up to have a go – and he nailed it! That contract value is now approaching one million dollars.

He could have thrown in the towel when he couldn't initially break through. He could have had a coach who said, 'Stuff it, you're not going to get this type of work.' But instead, I said to him, 'Just keep on knocking. Rejection is your best friend. You'll learn from this. What is the feedback you received? What changes are you going to make? What can you do to demonstrate the business in a different light? How can you give them the confidence that your business is more than capable of delivering the goods?'

Rejection is not a personal thing – it's a learning opportunity. If you go *"above the line"* (see chapter 15) and take ownership of the learning opportunity, you come back stronger and better and fitter than ever.

This can be a delicate balancing act though so be careful. There are three traps to avoid:

- **Don't annoy the potential client.** If they've made it extremely clear that you're not the right person to solve their frustration, that's fine. Don't push too hard. Let it go and move onto the next client. You won't win any friends by harassing people.

- **Don't chase clients who aren't right for you.** It's also important to recognise that they might have said no to you for a very good reason. You know who your target market is, right? Maybe this person is not in your target market. If that's the case, perhaps you're better off without them anyway. You build your business for the long term by attracting the right customers, not just any customers.

- **Don't take it personally.** It's all about business. You're not in this to be liked or popular, you're in it to make a profit, and you only do that by working with the right people and clients.

 **CHAPTER GEMS**

- Workflow is the life-blood of any business.

- There's no such thing as a bad business, only bad decisions.

- Make rejection your best friend.

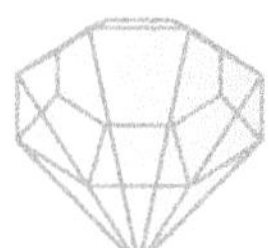

12. MANAGING YOUR ENVIRONMENT

WHO IS IN YOUR INNER CIRCLE?

Who you surround yourself with – both at work and away from work – is very important. The journey to business success can be long and winding, and the people in your inner circle need to be supporting you along the way. You must surround yourself with dream-makers, not dream-takers.

We all know who the dream-takers are. They are often people who are not happy with their own circumstances, so they're not going to be supportive of anybody else trying to reach their goals. Dream-takers will continually tell you you're not good enough, you're not smart enough, small business is too risky or that the whole thing is just plain stupid. Why would you hang around with such people?

You need to surround yourself with dream-makers. These

are people who will cheer you on from the sidelines, who understand what you are trying to do and have faith that you can achieve this. We all get energy from the people around us; if that energy is negative it can get in the way of your dreams, but having positive and supportive people around you will help carry you to your goals. Dream-makers will encourage you, support you, teach you and allow you to push your boundaries.

It is also imperative that you strategically surround yourself with the right people at work. I have a list of business associates that I study regularly to see how they could help me grow my business. Maybe it's somebody I could start a partnership with, or a client showing great potential for long-term growth. Every month I sit down with this list and identify and rank the 10 people who can most help me grow my business that month. Most months, two or three names on the list change or move up or down, and there are a few names that have been on the list for a long time.

This is a great habit for you to get into. You won't achieve success by yourself. So, why not strategically identify who you should be spending time with? Clearly identify the value these people provide to you and the outcomes they can help you with. How could you build a partnership with them? Who do they know who can help your business? What skills or knowledge do they have that you need? If you're not sure about something, ask them! Don't be shy. Turn it into a system. Like everything in your business, your approach to this needs to be systematic and quantifiable.

Here's the key to the success of this strategy; you have to help others in return. People will notice very quickly if you're trying to exploit them for your own gain. That's not the way to a profitable business, and it's also simply not a very nice thing to do. If you have an abundance mindset you'll know that there's plenty of success to go around. If you get out there and find people who can help you in your business and you do the same in return, everybody wins. I've found over my many years of business that just about everybody is happy to help if I'm willing to return the favour when the time comes.

So, at the start of each month, ask yourself the following big questions:

- Who are the 10 most influential people in your life and how can they help you?
- Who are the 10 most recent influential people you have helped and how have they helped you?

There are people who are already doing business with people you wish to do business with. Find out who they are. Find out what people are buying one step before you and one step after you. You then have the opportunity to bridge that gap and make it part of your inner circle. If you're a portrait photographer, a logical step before you would be a hairdresser, as people spruce themselves up before the shoot, and a logical step after you would be a framer. Ask yourself what opportunities this gives you to build your business, perhaps by creating partnerships with these people.

To help you meet more people who might be able to help your business it's vital that you take advantage of all business networking opportunities. You never know who you might meet and how they might be able to help. This is one of the reasons I started Board of Directors 12. We get together every fortnight. It's a great chance for everybody to receive support and encouragement and share skills and knowledge, and many of my clients make fantastic, mutually beneficial long-term connections. My grandfather used to say to me, 'Show me who your friends are and I'll show you with accuracy who *you* are.' He was a smart man.

Having such people in your life will also help to keep you accountable, and this is very important. Regular meetings mean regular chances to update them on your progress which can be a great cure for procrastination. And it's fine to pay somebody to help hold you accountable, such as a business coach. In fact, this can be a great motivator. I know people pay extra attention to things that I tell them when they are paying for the advice; free advice is much easier to ignore.

Keep all of this in mind when you meet somebody new. I recently gave a free consultation to a new client because I looked at his business and thought there would be great opportunities for us to work together in the future. Building a relationship is more important for the long-term success of my business than a one-off consultation fee.

Success leaves clues. Find out who you should be associating with and then make it happen with integrity first.

CHANGE THE PHYSICAL

We all know that our thoughts and feelings are both consciously and subconsciously influenced by our physical environment. It's why we feel relaxed sitting on a beach, or tense sitting in a traffic jam, or comfortable at home in familiar surrounds. The internal is very much influenced by the external.

Because of this, it's very important that you constantly look at your physical environment and see how it affects you. Do your surrounds reflect and encourage success? Are you portraying an image of professionalism? Or are you sitting at your desk in tracky dacks and an old T-shirt? If your environment doesn't have the look and feel of a successful business it will be more difficult for you to *be* a successful business. If your office or store is cluttered and disorganised it will be difficult for you to run a tight ship. If you can't even tidy the office people won't expect much from you, and if they don't expect much from you you're not going to be able to lead them.

Your environment also needs to reflect what stage you are at with your business. For example, I recently expanded and took over the office next door because we needed the extra room. As we have grown we also outgrew our space. If you are trying to sign a $1 million client you are not going to get far having meetings at your kitchen table. Your physical environment needs to be congruent with your plans and expectations for your business.

EXERCISE: Changing your physical environment

Have a look around your workplace. List five ways that you could improve the physical environment so that it better reflects the standards and expectations of your business.

1. ____

2. ____

3. ____

4. ____

5. ____

Marking occasions

I also think it's very important to mark occasions and turning points in your business with physical changes. If you reach your goal of signing a $200,000 client, mark the occasion! Buy yourself a new chair, or put a new picture on the wall, or throw out the rickety shelf that has been annoying you. Such physical statements of success are both a celebration of what you've done and a motivator to do more. Every morning when you sit in that new chair you'll be reminded of how it feels to achieve one of your goals, and this will help spur you on to the next one. If you mentally feel good and feel motivated to keep going because of the physical change this will help to keep you on track.

EXERCISE: Celebrating goals

List three goals you have in the coming months, large or small. Make a plan for how you will celebrate these goals when they are reached.

1. ____________________________________

2. ____________________________________

3. ____________________________________

What else is going on in your life?

It can also be very valuable to have a look at everything else you are doing in your life. Anything that affects you physically or emotionally will have an effect on your business. Is there anything that is holding you back? Are you getting enough exercise? Is your diet good? Do you get enough sleep? What TV shows are you watching? What do you do on your weekends? To achieve your dreams you need to be alert, healthy, on the ball and physically up to it.

EXERCISE: What's holding you back?

List three things that you are not happy with in your life outside of work, and why. Make a plan for how you are going to change these things. And then do it!

1. ____

   I can fix this by: _______________________________

2. ____

   I can fix this by: _______________________________

3. ____

   I can fix this by: _______________________________

EXERCISE: The bucket list

Do you know what a bucket list is? It's a list of things you really want to do in life before you kick the bucket! Too many of us are going to 'get around' to doing these things, and they never happen. Have you always wanted to jump out of an aeroplane? Have you always wanted to climb a mountain? Run a marathon? Learn to play guitar? Learn another language? Remember, it's not just about work, it's about quality of life. Write down three things on your bucket list, and a date they will be done by. And remember, 'next year' never comes.

1. _____________________________ Date: __________

2. _____________________________ Date: __________

3. _____________________________ Date: __________

ALL FIRED UP...

By now you should be starting to see the path that will take your business from deadwood to diamond. You should be all fired up as it's starting to dawn on you that maybe your business isn't deadwood after all. How exciting!

I've had clients who came to me lost and bewildered because

they couldn't find a way through. They had all the will in the world but they were lacking the skills and knowledge they needed to turn things around. Nothing gives me greater satisfaction than seeing them a few months later, beaming from ear to ear because they have found a way forward and they now have confidence and clarity about where they are going and how they are going to get here. That's my A to B. That's the bridge I build.

When you've finished reading this page I want you to close your eyes for a minute and think about your goals. What's your big dream? A trip to New York? A new Porsche? To help 1,000 people in your community gain employment? To take the family around Australia? Move to a house by the beach? Donate $50,000 to your favourite charity every year?

Imagine what it would be like to live that dream.

Think about walking down Fifth Avenue. What can you see? What do you hear? Can you smell the hot dogs being sold on the street corners? Can you hear the constant hum of the traffic?

What colour is that Porsche going to be? Imagine unlocking it and sitting in it for the first time. The new car smell. The leather seats. The Porsche logo on the steering wheel. Picture it parked in front of your house and the sound it makes when you fire it up.

Imagine the ripple effect if you help 1,000 people gain employment. Think about how many lives that would touch.

How much do you want it?

What would you do to achieve this dream?

What *will* you do to achieve this dream?

If you take your business from deadwood to diamond it can be yours. The only thing standing in the way is you.

Remember: **Get brilliant at the basics.**

 ## CHAPTER GEMS

- The journey to business success can be long and winding, and the people in your inner circle need to be supporting you along the way.
- The internal is very much influenced by the external.
- Imagine what it would be like to live your dream.

CASE STUDY: Pinnacle Health Club

Pinnacle Health Club is a privately-owned, full service 24/7 health club located in the Eastern suburbs of Melbourne. It has three, soon to be four, locations. It is currently operating in an industry experiencing high growth from both increasing trends in health and fitness lifestyles, as well as rapid expansion from chains, including full-service clubs, as well as no-frills 24/7 chains. It is an industry where clients are spoilt with choice for options, and retention is a key driver for continued success. It's an industry where to stay ahead of the market, or sometimes just to stay afloat, Pinnacle needs to be continually reinvesting in each of their clubs' physical and online space, as well as constantly developing their staff and keeping up with technological trends. Let's hear their story.

1. What problems were you facing in your business?

We had a lack of direction and focus and were confused about what our growth goals should be for business. We were spread between three different industries and three completely different businesses. We were also still very much bogged down in the day-to-day operations, making it difficult for us to focus and spend time on business improvement and development.

2. Why do you think these problems occurred?

We hadn't defined, or communicated our set roles and responsibilities with ourselves and our staff. Often our staff didn't know who to call or go to, depending on the question or problem. We were constantly receiving calls/emails from staff and our managers. I remember one particular day where I received seven calls in two hours from one manager. It largely came down to us not training our managers to the best of their ability and allowing them to have decision-making rights that freed us up from the day-to-day operations. We were struggling to delegate authority and responsibilities to our many capable staff.

We also lacked attention in our strategic planning and

forecasting. We failed to measure our initiatives and therefore identify what areas worked better than others.

3. What was holding you back?

Spreading ourselves too thin, confidence, requesting and allowing our team members to step up and be a part of the business decision-making and growth. Ultimately we were still very much in the day-to-day running of the business, which didn't leave much time for anything else.

We were also arguing and butting heads a lot as a couple. We are very competitive which, when directed appropriately, works really well for us and pushes us to achieve great things together, but when directed at each other, raises alarm bells.

4. At what point did you recognise that you needed help, and what motivated you to get it?

Working with Stefan has transformed our business, and ourselves, as business owners and leaders. At first we were hesitant to work with a business coach, particularly given our lack of knowledge and emphasis on personal development and training to date. We were getting complacent and caught up in the day-to-day running of our businesses, and we struggled with clarity and direction. But we didn't think we needed help, or at least didn't see the benefit or value of a business coach.

This attitude was largely created from an experience we had had with another business coach a year prior. We had met a business coach for an initial consultation and he was an epic fail. He took the tact of trying to bully us into coaching by pointing out how young and 'inexperienced' we were, not recognising what we had achieved to date. He played on the young and vulnerable fear factor, and essentially suggested that we needed him otherwise we would make terrible mistakes. But that wasn't us and it put us off coaching.

Then we met Stefan at a client Christmas party for our mutual bank and he invited us to a "tasting session". During this session, we realised quickly that he inspired us and got us excited about the possibilities for us and our business. Unfortunately, Ben spent most of the time thinking of ways he could help the other business owners in the room, rather than focusing on our own business. So we decided that one-on-one coaching would be a great start. Our initial concern was the financial investment, but seven months down the track, we don't even notice that line on our P&L, and the returns far outweigh the cost anyway. Our mindset is now that it's an investment into us and our future, not an expense.

What attracted us to Stefan the most was that he backs himself 100%. He says it like it is. He is a true inspiration and he is also trying to grow and develop his own business as well. The final overriding factor was the idea of a support person and encouragement from an experienced businessman. It can be a lonely place, running your own business, and a coach can fill that gap.

5. What did you learn that helped you solve these problems?

- Our new mantra – 'do one thing and do it well'! Last year we had three gyms, as well as three other peripheral businesses in completely different industries, largely to satisfy Ben's entrepreneurial spirit, but also due to a lack of strategic direction. We are now getting out of the outside three businesses to focus on our core business of the health clubs.
- Always put back into your team with constant training and development. Our new focus on this has not only allowed us to step out of the day-to-day operations, but it has seen a shift in excitement from our team for their future career opportunities, and increased motivation and production levels. We are experiencing synergies never seen before for idea generation and new initiatives or programs.
- Reporting and score-carding on an ongoing basis – this helps us identify the fluctuations of our business on a weekly basis, and assists in developing a more predictable flow of cash and ultimately a better profit margin.

- Identifying areas of the business that are 100% not negotiable.
- Systems, systems and systems – dummy-proof our procedures to allow our staff to feel more supported and to ensure the experience and culture at each of our gyms is the same for our members.

6. What systems have you put in place that have helped your business?

We have redefined our own responsibilities so that we are no longer stepping on each other's toes. This has also eliminated the confusion our team had with whom to report to or whom to contact. We have redefined our Club Managers' roles and provided them with more authority for decision-making, allowing them to be the true leader of their teams.

Stefan has turned us into coaches for our team. Our entire team is now on the same page, everyone knows where we are going, and is consistently stepping up and excelling in their roles. In turn, this has enabled us to work 'on' rather than 'in' our business. As a result, we now involve them in strategic planning and business improvement. Through this collaboration and support, we have experienced great synergies with 50 heads being better than 1! Plus the vibe is excitement all around, as our team see opportunities and career progression for themselves as well. They are all part of our journey and everyone is loving it and embracing what's next to come.

We document all of our procedures and processes to make the business streamlined, to provide governance, support for training, and to enable further growth.

We provide focus sheets for our managers to increase accountability to them, as well as to allow them to focus on three to four goals each month that are hopefully more interesting to them than their normal weekly 'chores'.

We have introduced increased communication. We hold weekly

meetings with our managers that are structured and chaired by a different person each week. We also have monthly meetings with our staff that are held by our club managers at each location.

7. What was the biggest single change you made to yourself or your business that helped turn things around?

We found clarity and direction. We needed to take a step back to move two steps forward.

8. What other changes have you made and how have they helped?

Stefan has made us accountable through asking the 'hard questions', regular catch ups, focus sheets and KPI reports. We now have greater visibility over the performance of our business from the KPIs and finances, something we very much lacked.

9. What fears or challenges did you have to overcome? How did you do this?

Letting go of control in areas and trusting our team with our business was a major challenge. We did this by identifying areas where they could make mistakes, and letting them.

10. What advice do you have for other small business owners who are currently struggling?

Stefan is an inspiration and provides a great deal of motivation to us as leaders. As a business owner, it can be at times a lonely position, but with Stefan as our business coach, we feel we have someone who supports us, who in turn is a business success in his own right, and as such, knows his stuff.

It's always the cost that is of most concern to a business. It was to us and we were already making good profits, so to a struggling business we can only imagine how much of a stumbling block the cost of coaching could be. But we have never looked back and soon realised that the returns were not just financial, they were also personal/intrinsic as well. We come out of each of our sessions motivated and ready to take on the world!

PLUS Stefan guarantees at least a 10 times return on investment! Which we have achieved – and more!

11. How is your business performing now? Has this exceeded your expectations?

With Stefan on our side, we definitely feel we have made significant progress with our team and streamlining our processes. We know we are making the right decisions with Stefan as our mentor.

12. What specific goals in dollar terms have you achieved from implementing the changes you have made

We achieved 20% greater profit for FY13 than we had targeted for.

13. What specific non-monetary achievements have you achieved?

We now work together better than we ever did, which naturally helps our home life. Work/life balance is still not quite where we want it to be, but we see a light at the end of the tunnel, and we are not far away from it. As a husband and wife team we now work much better together, which is the most significant difference to us.

14. What changes do you still need to make to your business, and why?

We need to:

- Change over systems and implement new procedures – this has been in the pipeworks since the start of the year, but needs to be implemented in a timely manner to spend time training staff and to minimise any negative impact across all locations. We need to test the waters first at one location, before rolling it out across them all. Unfortunately, these things cannot be done overnight. Documenting the systems and procedures took four months alone.

- Implement our new retention program (this comes after the systems). We developed this program along with our emerging leaders, and it will be implemented as soon as the systems have been changed over.

- Further develop our emerging leaders – create 2ICs at each gym to allow for future growth and staff taking leave, etc. Work on building our staff's strengths, and supporting them with someone else who complements their weaknesses.

15. Where do you think your business will be in five years time?

Our business will be solid, with a great team working behind it, no longer relying on us. We will have grown in numbers to be a well recognised brand in the eastern and south eastern suburbs, and will have a business that in good will, is worth 5 fold in profits. We will also have consolidated some of our business debt to investment debt and risk share.

16. If you hadn't made an effort to get help, where do you think you would be right now?

We would still be spreading ourselves across our six businesses, rather than having a strong and shared focus on our direction. We most likely would not have been in a position to purchase our fourth location from a time and management perspective.

17. What are your top five tips for other business owners?

- Always have an internal focus and develop your team. Without them, you cannot be a success.
- Have clear goals and direction.
- Report and measure often.
- Be passionate about what you do, work hard but have fun as well.
- Celebrate your successes.

18. What big goal have you recently achieved in your business?

We have just purchased our fourth gym.

19. What big goal have you recently achieved in your life?

We have purchased our dream home in our dream location – at the age of 26!

Part 4: Carat

" The first rule of any technology used in a business is that automation applied to an efficient operation will magnify the efficiency. The second is that automation applied to an inefficient operation will magnify the inefficiency. ""

—Bill Gates

The size and depth of a small business is its true value in its discipline to sweat the small stuff. It's the consistency of improvement that builds the ultimate foundation for growth.

When it comes to diamonds, carats are measured in units of two milligrams. How small is that? Well, a grain of rice weighs around 20 milligrams – that should give you an idea! So carats are extremely small, but the more carats a diamond has the more valuable it is. Your business is no different: the small stuff will contribute greatly to your profits. It's about shaping and refining your business for the long term, and putting your stake in the ground and saying this is who we are and what we do and this is why you should be choosing us. It's about being in growth mode all the time, about having a plan B, and making sure you are always moving forward. It's about always striving to be your best.

Everything you do in your business needs to fit in with your strategic plan, even the little things. There are a whole lot of little things and if you add them all up they make a very big difference.

So, make sure you sweat the small stuff!

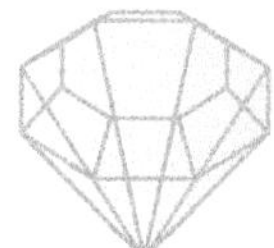

13. GROWTH MODE

MAINTENANCE MODE VS GROWTH MODE

Have a think about your approach to your business right now. Are you in maintenance mode or growth mode? Which of these two do you connect with? You must look in the mirror and make a conscious choice about this because they are two different mindsets and whichever approach you take will affect each and every decision you make in your business. If you're not clear about which mode you are in you could be headed for trouble.

Given you are trying to take your business from deadwood to diamond, which mindset do you think will serve you best? You may think you should be in maintenance mode, treading carefully and being conservative until you can get back on your feet, and then you can worry about growth. But let me tell you something right now; you should *always* be in growth mode. That's right, always.

To be in growth mode means you are focused on the future. You should have five-year and ten-year goals and shorter term targets along the way that you know will get you there. Being in growth mode means having a strategic plan that is the basis for all the decisions you make. It means having the right staff who will grow with you, and the right physical environment that takes into account your future needs so you won't have to scramble together unsatisfactory solutions at the last minute. Always remember that the short term is just a step on the journey to long term, so you must always be clear on your destination. Sometimes you must go two steps backwards to go four steps forward, but you must see the opportunities before you and not just the costs. Focus on the *cost of opportunity*, not the *cost of growth*, and be prepared to take a short-term hit for long-term gain.

Four key areas

Being in growth mode means looking at four key areas when you make any decisions. Every choice you make in your business must conform to your strategic plans for:

- sales
- marketing
- operations
- finance.

As an example, if you are making plans to increase your leads, let's see how that fits with these areas.

Circles of Strategic Alignment

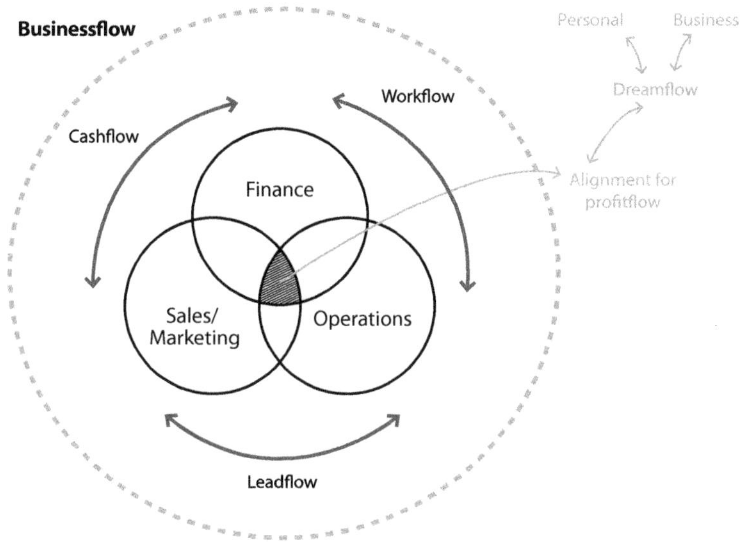

Finance is easy. What will it cost for you to increase your leads? Is that in accordance with your finance plans? How much are you prepared to invest? Can you afford that right now? Do you have the required cashflow? What are your strategies and allowable costs to buy customers? And if you are successful in buying these customers, are you in a position to invest in the resources and expand as needed to meet this growth? Will there be enough cash left over after you have bought these customers to service them and still leave a profit? New customers are not the same as profit. Being busy is not the same as profit. Putting an ad on TV is not the same as profit. The only thing that is the same as profit is…profit!

Does what you are doing fit with your sales and marketing plans? If you start getting more leads, will your sales team be equipped to handle them? Every time you create a lead, how will your sales structure help your future client to move along? How do you help them by making your stuff easy to buy, so that they will discriminate in your favour? How are you increasing loyalty? Are you creating clients for life? Are you losing money on the first sale or making money? Either answer is okay as long as it's in accordance with your plan. Creating loss leaders can be a great tactic if your clients have a high life-time value. You should always be thinking about more than just securing the next sale. You should be thinking about the one after, and the next one, and the one after that, and on and on it goes…

If you are successful in generating more leads, and your sales team or structure are successful in converting these leads into paying customers, it is then critical that you have the operations and systems in place to delight these clients. At what stage will you need more resources and people? Just securing their business is not enough; you have to follow through with exceptional service. That's how you build sustainable profits.

Every decision you make – *every* decision – must be made in accordance with your long-term strategic plan. Earlier in the book we talked about pilots flying from Melbourne to London. When they taxi away from the gate all they want to do is make it to the start of the runway, and when they make it to the start of the runway their sole focus is on taking off. The pilot isn't worried about lining up at the gate at Heathrow when he takes off at Tullamarine, but he still ends up at the right destination because each and every decision made along the way has the ultimate goal in mind. If the pilot were to take off with no flight plan and just head in the general direction of London, the chances of arriving at the right destination would be rather slim.

Is that what you are doing in your business? Because if it is, you won't get where you should be going either.

In case of emergency, break glass

Do you come up with a plan B only when plan A has collapsed? When things start to go pear-shaped do you start making decisions in a blind panic just to get out of the current mess? This is a great way to relieve the stress of running a small business, because if you keep doing this, fairly soon you won't have a small business left to worry about.

Just as important as using your plan to guide your decisions and growth is having a plan B for everything you do. We all know that despite best efforts and careful planning things still go wrong from time to time. All businesses hit speed bumps. It's inevitable. So whenever you make an important decision in your business, make sure you have a backup plan as well. If you're planning a new advertising campaign and expect to attract 2,000 new customers, what happens if you only get 200? What happens if your new product gets overtaken by the competition 16 minutes after it comes out? What will you do if one of your suppliers goes bust the day before you're expecting a major delivery?

You need to have contingencies planned for things that could conceivably go wrong in your business. And these plans need to be viable as well. Don't dismiss your contingency plans because you think they are unlikely to be needed. Most of the time they won't be, but from time to time they will, and you have to stay on track even when you revert to plan B. If you can't come up with a viable plan B that fits with your strategic plan, the solution is simple: you can't do plan A.

It's crucial for you to think about what unexpected events could come along to disrupt your progress. For each strategic decision you make, you must work out:

- what you are going to do
- what you are expecting to happen as a result
- what it is that you don't know about this decision that could blindside you.

Too many business owners only consider the first two of these and not the third. They don't think about the worst-case scenario. You must be comfortable not only with the worst-case scenario of plan A but the worst-case scenario of plan B. If you know the worst-case scenario for plan B and your business will be okay if this happens, think about how much confidence you'll have pursuing plan A!

We all know that the vast majority of the time the worst-case scenario for plan B *doesn't* happen, but we also know that sometimes it *does*, so you need to know what it is and be ready for it.

EXERCISE: Plan B

Have a look at the crucial systems in your business and the major decisions you make. Do you have backup plans in place for these? If not, write down a possible backup plan for each item, and then research this plan further. What is the worst-case scenario for this plan B? What would happen if this were to occur? Does this make you think twice about what you are doing? Ultimately, if you are okay with the worst-case scenario for Plan B, then Plan A is ready to go.

What if...

Make this your favourite question: 'What if...' Challenge your own decisions mercilessly. Do they fit your plan? Do they REALLY fit your plan? Really? Or are you just doing something for the sake of it and you haven't really thought it through? Non-strategic thinking leads to knee-jerk reactions and bad decisions, and this does not lead to growth. If you keep pouring more time, energy and money into your business without stepping back and taking stock, you'll end up with a huge mortgage, lots of grey hairs and some not-so-fond memories of that time you once started a business.

EXERCISE: What if?

Have a look at the next major decision you are going to make today and ask 'what if?' List at least three things that could go wrong with this decision. What is your plan B if this occurs?

Can I see you in my office?

It's also at this point you must understand that if you are in growth mode you need to take great care about who you have on your team. This is something you need to get control of right now because it's vital to the success of your business. You can't and won't grow without the right people around you. This will be discussed more later.

So how do I stay in growth mode?

You need to be driven to be in growth mode. It's not for the faint-hearted. It's about *going to*, it's not *waiting for*. You must make it happen, not wait for it to happen. Some people seem to just plod through life waiting for the day they win the lotto. That attitude is not going to cut it here. You're either all in or you're out.

Here are the top six most important aspects of staying in growth mode:

♦ **You have to be growth-minded – always!** This is not optional. I meet business owners all the time who are happy to have a growth attitude when things are booming but switch to maintenance mode when times seem tough. Wrong! If you have a growth attitude, have strategic planning in place, know your market and where you are going there is no need to become conservative when times get tough. In fact, it's imperative that you are in growth mode when this happens. We'll look at this more later.

- **Focus on the basics.** Keep things simple and focus on executing well. Make sure your team has this attitude too, both your internal team and any support you outsource.

- **Have effective communications systems.** You need to have effective systems in place that allow you to communicate quickly and easily with your current and future clients. These days everybody is hung up on Facebook, Twitter and the like, and they can be powerful tools, but always keep in mind the goal is *effective communication* not just being popular.

- **Have effective operating cashflow management.** This is vital. Without this I can just about guarantee you will not survive. It doesn't matter how many clients you have or how great your products are, if you can't pay your bills you are going out of business.

- **Manage the hard decisions.** When it's time, you need to wield the axe. You are the leader in your business and that comes with the responsibility to make tough decisions. You need to embrace this mindset. It's part of your responsibility as leader of the business. If you don't accept this role, your hesitation and inconsistency when making decisions will cause confusion and this will cause you to fail. If you can't do it, how can you expect your staff to? If you can't manage this you shouldn't be in business. (Brutal truth, remember?)

- **Create a positive environment.** If you operate in fear of losing clients, if you don't back yourself, if you don't go to the cliff's edge, if you don't do the things that separate you from the competition, if you don't push yourself and your business to be the best you can be, you will die. If you operate with a positive outlook and an attitude of abundance you can thrive and grow.

What about when times get tough?

When I tell business owners that they *always* need to be in growth mode, they often ask me, 'But what about when times are tough?' My response is: 'Which part of *always* did you not understand?' Too many business owners allow themselves to be a victim of the environment around them. If you have built a robust business, you know your market intimately and what clients want from you, and you know how to deliver it, tough times will bring you no fear.

Let's use my own business as an example. I know that in Australia there are 2.2 million small businesses that have an ABN and are turning over between $700,000 to $2 million a year. That's a huge target market! And I want to serve 1,000 of them a month. Have a think about that. That's 0.045% of the market. That constitutes great success for my business. I know this because I've done my numbers and my planning. So let's say the economy slows down a bit and some small businesses close their doors. Let's say that after a couple of years of recession there are only 2 million small businesses in Australia. How much does that affect me? Now I'm after 0.050% of the market – not much difference is there? If I wake up each day and have 2 million potential clients out there – game on! That's awesome! What recession?

Let's have another look at The Drain Man from an earlier case study. During the GFC several years ago, plumbers weren't getting enough work on construction sites and so they were starting to do drain clearing for ridiculously cheap prices because they didn't have any other work. The Drain Man had at his point elevated the industry, but suddenly he was competing with these guys who were fighting for a dollar. He lost a bit of market share. What did he do? He could have dropped the quality of his own services and then dropped his prices in an effort to compete, but instead he stuck to his guns and started knocking on the door of some potential A-grade clients. He had to go backwards to go forward, but by continuing his high-quality presence and marketing strategy of being the go-to guy for drain clearing, he didn't need 200 jobs every day, just 20 good ones.

Sometimes when things get tough people automatically turn to survival tactics, without a strategy or belief that they are better than this. Yes, we need to get through tough times, but we don't need to throw out all our hard work and forget who we are and what we do. You may have to take a job with lower profitability to get you through the month, but don't throw everything out and make this your long-term strategy. Before you know it you'll be in a pool of sharks and you'll get eaten. When they zig, you have to zag.

If you're an A-grade business you know where the diamonds are, and you just need a handful of them. You need to be clear about your market size and then compare that to your goals, and know the direct relationship between them.

When you've found the right target market and know your numbers, tough times won't worry you.

And here's another thing to think about: when times are bad, some of your competitors will close their doors. If you're a roof tiler, there might not be as many houses being built, but are there going to be *no* houses built? Of course not! People will still need roofs on houses, just not as many. So who is going to go out of business? Those that lack clarity, don't have strategic plans in place, don't know who their target market is or how to reach them, those who switch to maintenance mode at signs of trouble and don't have solid financial and operating foundations in place will go belly up. If you want to come out the other side, make sure this isn't you! Don't run for the hills with your white flag. Let everybody else do that. You'll be the one left standing – and thriving.

Having a growth mindset at such times is just as important as when things are going well. You've made your plan – stick to it. Think about our pilots flying to London. If they encounter a storm along the way and have to adjust their course, they don't then say, 'Hey, now I guess we're going to Paris'. They know where they are going and they stick to their destination. Their plans for the flight have taken into account that there might be storms along the way so they are not knocked off course.

When the economy looks shaky or a business runs into trouble the knee-jerk response of many business owners – small or large – is to cut costs, and usually this is done by cutting staff and closing stores. But cutting expenses will *never* get you out of a hole, it will just confirm that your business is going in the wrong direction. If you have the right people around you, how does getting rid of them help your business?

The other reflexive response is to throw money into advertising, but again this doesn't help, it just makes the business owner feel like they are 'doing something'. But throwing $10,000 at an ill-conceived and desperate ad campaign won't get you the customers you need. It's a sign of a business that doesn't know who its target market is or how to reach them. That's not a focused business plan; that's pin the tail on the donkey.

Growth mode is about planning, and maintenance is not planning.

Are you at your full potential? It's not about who is the smartest, it's about recognising the void and filling it. I've seen plenty of people smarter than I am fail at running businesses.

When the opportunity moves from the head to the heart you will move forward. When you fully own and take responsibility for what you are doing, and when you are totally committed, good things will start to happen.

The imaginary CEO

This is an exercise I love to do with my clients. Have a think about this: if you hired a new CEO or GM, what would you expect this person to deliver in accordance with the size of the market you are in? What would success look like? What growth would you expect? What percentage or number of clients would you expect over the next year, two years, five years? Be specific. Think about it and write down some numbers.

Now, here's the kicker: what goals do you have for *yourself*? Are they the same? If not, *why not*? If you're running the business, why don't you have these high expectations of yourself? Why do you think somebody else could do better than you can? If your goals for the imaginary CEO were bigger than your goals for yourself, you have a problem. In fact, you *are* the problem. Until your goals and expectations of yourself are much bigger you will get in the way. You won't allow other resources, people or structures to come into your business to allow it to reach its full potential, and you won't be able to push the people you do have to achieve their personal best.

Education and growth

Motivation by itself is not enough to ensure the prosperity of your business; people need to be educated. You and your staff need to learn the fundamentals of running a business. You need to move from just being a plumber to being somebody who is running a plumbing business, from an accountant to somebody who is running an accounting practice, from an editor to somebody who is running a publishing business. Your expertise in your field is most likely what got you started, and that's great, but you must move above and beyond this to achieve long-term success and growth.

The reason many people are happy to stay in mediocrity is they don't know what they don't know. They think they've reached their full potential already because they don't know what else is out there. They don't know that abundant opportunities are just around the corner. But the real problem comes when people learn what they could and should be doing and still do nothing about it. This is known as *conscious incompetence*: 'I now know what I don't know'. If you choose to do nothing at this point then this is where your business will start to falter. This is where you miss the opportunity to grow.

The more educated you are, the more motivated you will be to get great results and the more you will have the capacity to do that. If you have become more skilled and more knowledgeable you will be able to see the path ahead, and this provides its own motivation. This becomes a cycle of positive reinforcement that leads to even better results.

When you hit a glass ceiling this indicates a need for more education. When you reach a point of frustration and you truly want to grow but you don't know how, it's time for more learning. And whatever stage you are at, there is *always* more to learn. You will never 'make it'. The moment you think you have 'made it' is the moment you and your business start going backwards. I have more to learn. We all do.

Are you at your full potential right now?

Growth and the myth of work/life balance

People often say they started their own business with the aim of achieving better 'work/life balance', only to find after six months that this is an unattainable myth sold to us by the media and 'experts' who actually know nothing of running a business.

You know I prefer brutal truth to just telling you what you want to hear, so here we go again: when you are growing a business, work/life balance just ain't going to happen. Sorry. Are you saying you want to work until 3 pm every day, except for Wednesdays when you want to knock off at 1.47 pm so you can walk in the park just when the sun is shining through the trees? Good luck with that. Want to start at 9.30 am every other day so you can fit in that yoga class? Great – but it's going to cost your business.

Now, don't get me wrong, I'm all about your business doing well so you can enjoy the other things in life. There is nothing – *absolutely nothing* – more important to me than spending time with my wife and kids. I work hard in my business so that I can do that. As I write this my family are overseas. They've gone on ahead of me and I'm going to catch up with them in Greece. I'm putting in ten days straight now to get on top of things before I go, and I'm okay with that because I know at the end I'm out of here and I get to spend some wonderful time with my family.

The thought that you can tailor your business around your personal life and have them fit together *just so* has got many a business owner into trouble. It's about personal alignment. Your personal life must be aligned with your goals and your dreams. That includes your family, friends, pets, social commitments – whatever is going on in your life. It's your job to make it all fit together. Without this personal alignment, professional alignment won't happen. No one reaches success without sacrifice. The more you have alignment and harmony the more you will be able to achieve.

Business is demanding. It always has been and it always will be. There are no magic tricks and no short-cuts to success, so you have to be prepared to do whatever it takes. Hard work and effort need to be part of your routine. If you knock off at 3 o'clock every day to pick the kids up from school, how on earth are you going to motivate the staff who are staying at the office? Do you think they are going to power on until 5 pm, or be on Facebook at 3.01 pm? If you're close to signing a major client and they want to meet at 8 am, are you going to say no because you have yoga?

So if work/life balance is a myth, what is possible? I prefer to aim for work/life *harmony*. That means you recognise that sometimes your business must be the priority. Sometimes there will be late nights (or even *all* nighters), and weekends and early starts. That's just part of the process when you are building a business. The reason you do this is to make your business successful and the reason you want your business to be successful is so that down the road you will have more time and more freedom to do the things you really want to do.

You have to do whatever it takes to make your business strong, and then you can back off a little. Whenever your business needs you, you must be there. But when your plan allows for time off, because you have great systems and great people in place, that's when you get to relax. One of my aims for my business is to never work another month of August in my life. That's right. Never. I'm not there yet but I'm close. So, right now, I'm working really hard to achieve that goal. The effort comes now, the reward later.

It's not about 50% work, 50% family, or whatever other percentage you come up with. Sometimes it will be 100% work and at other times 100% family. The key to managing this is that the people around you understand this and support you in what you do. It's about you managing their expectations and explaining to them what you are doing and why, and that if you are working hard now it's so that you can have the rewards later. Nothing can undo a business quicker than an unsupportive spouse or family; believe me, I've seen it happen too many times. If your personal life isn't aligned with your dreams and your goals for your business you're going to have a problem. You need to talk to your family. If your family is not a support structure but a problem you are doomed.

How much more do I need to do?

If you have kids you know this question well: *are we there yet?* I hear this from my kids whenever we go for a long journey in the car. I also hear this all the time from my clients: *how much more?* The simple answer to this is that *you are never done building your business*. There will be some periods where growth is stronger than others, but from the day you start your business to the day you leave you should be trying to make it bigger and better.

If you're feeling a little overwhelmed, here's a great exercise that can help you clear the decks a little bit. It's called the **Traffic Light Exercise**. For many clients I find that this is a moment of truth and a moment of clarity. It's actually very simple, but also very powerful. Simply answer the following questions:

* What three things do you need to **stop** doing?
* What three things do you need to **continue** doing?
* What three things do you need to **start** doing?

You can begin this activity by looking at yourself. Everything you do in your business must be led by you. What do *you* need to stop, start and continue? Look at your default diary. What are the three key things to achieve today rather than the 50 trivial things to do?

Then look at your business and then your staff and departments. This will have a snowball effect, as your business does away with unnecessary tasks and spends more time on more valuable activities.

For each activity you do, ask yourself if what you are doing is relevant to:

- your customers
- your industry
- your community
- you and your life purpose.

How frequently are you being relevant for these areas? And if something is not relevant, why are you doing it at all? This is another time for brutal truth. If you're not leading like this your staff won't follow. This is why you start with yourself.

At some point you become more aware of the stuff you are doing on a reactive versus proactive basis. What are the majority of your activities right now? What is the business owner's work versus employees' work ratio looking like right now for you? What are *you* doing that should be done by one of your staff? Sometimes it's about stopping stuff rather than starting stuff. This has a massive impact on growth and breaking through.

Breaking through

We all know what it's like to be under the pump, to feel like we're being pushed and pulled in a million directions and can't see the way ahead. The only way to break through when things get like this is to apply pressure.

There are two types of pressure you can apply: negative and positive.

Negative pressure is where you get pushed to breaking point because you feel as if you are stuck. You don't know what you don't know. You can't see the next step. If you feel like this, you have two choices: you either run away, or hang around and get through this emotion to the point of breakthrough.

Consider this situation like a pot of boiling water. When pressure is applied – in the form of heat – you keep on going until you are pushed to your limit. At this point you are simmering. At this point you are perturbed, and you have two choices. You can stay under pressure on the stove, or get out and relax again off the stove. Most people will run from this pressure and therefore they never grow. If you stay in the pressure you will become more and more perturbed until you break through – and when you do you will pop through and release energy and emotion. This could be tears, laughter, anger – whatever it takes to push you forward. To achieve this breakthrough you have to *break up* what's not working for you, you have to *break with* old habits that weren't moving you forward. You have to *break away* from people and environments that are no good for you and you have to *break down* exactly where you are right now. To get to the point where this happens you have to be able to handle the heat on the stove until it gets to simmering. It's not always easy. Everybody goes through pain.

Negative pressure holds us back because we are not skilled enough or strong enough to deal with it, so we live an unfulfilling life. Instead of hanging around and facing the issues, people run, and so their problems never go away. Until you *break up, break with, break away* and *break down*, you won't go anywhere.

Positive pressure is deciding that you are going for it. You create goals and decide that you are all in. Setting targets and having planned activities to reach them creates positive pressure that will pull you forward. It's forging ahead with a clear destination and a plan to get you there. It's doing the chosen and planned activities to reach your targets. This is growth mode pressure that helps you shape your diamond. It's about being just behind your identity and consistently pushing yourself forward. Stretching your identity provides positive pressure. Otherwise life's good, so why would you forge ahead? There's no positive pressure.

You can't get to positive pressure without getting rid of negative pressure first, so your initial task is to deal with whatever issues you are facing now before you try to move on. Once you have cleared away the negative you can start thinking long term and stay aligned to your strategic plan. You can focus on the actions you need to be committed to. You won't be forced to make hasty decisions to avert the latest calamity.

Long-term thinking

Key to developing positive pressure in your business is basing your decisions on long-term thinking. The challenge with long-term thinking is that it requires creative energy and an outside-the-box approach. It requires a commitment to high energy. Your level of thinking is just as important as what you do. If your goal is massive then your business will become massive, but if you think small then that's where you'll stay.

You need to be thinking about how you can be in the top 10% in your industry. How can you make the competition irrelevant? How can you be the benchmark? What are you doing consistently right? What are you doing wrong, and what are you doing about this?

Flexibility

Sweating the small stuff is critical to being flexible.

You need flexibility in a market that's moving up or down. In a market where the big boys are laying off staff, customers will start getting frustrated because they are used to dealing with somebody who is no longer there. And when things change quickly – as they do these days – larger companies have trouble responding. They are victims of their own size and unwieldy systems and operations.

The inflexibility of large organisations provides opportunities and advantages for small and medium operators. If you are flexible and can react rapidly to changes you will be able to grow your market share by offering big-business service with small business flexibility. You can jump in and fill a gap while the big boys are still having meetings to decide if the gap exists. You won't get caught up in your own red tape and miss opportunities for profits and market share. You can look at your scoreboard and have vital data about what is going on, and immediately know whether what you are doing is working and respond appropriately. You can take action today, not in three months time.

 ## CHAPTER GEMS

- Are you in maintenance mode or growth mode?
- Every choice you make in your business must conform to your strategic plans for sales and marketing, operations and finance.
- Just as important as using your plan to guide your decisions and growth is having a plan B for everything you do.
- The only way to break through when things get tough is to apply pressure.

14. STAYING IN TOUCH

I HAVE 1,490,987,765,123 LIKES ON FACEBOOK

You need to be tech savvy these days. It's essential. Not being on Facebook or Twitter or LinkedIn is like not having a mobile phone or still using a fax machine. It makes you look hopelessly out of date. But how do you measure the success of your online systems? Is it the number of hits? Numbers of friends, followers, likers, whatevers? Number of comments you get on your posts?

Have a good, hard think about the things we've looked at so far in this book, and then answer this for me: how is online different from any other aspect of your business? Despite what many people believe, it isn't. It's not about likes or friends. It's not a 'new economy'.

So the answer is as dull and boring as it is obvious: you measure your online success by how much money it puts in the bank.

Seriously, you expected anything else?

We've all heard the boasts before. I have 27,000 followers on Facebook. I come up first on Google. I get re-tweeted more than Pink. Let me have a look at my accounting software and see where I enter the number of likes I have on Facebook…hmmm…can't see it. Let's see where my Google ranking goes on my balance sheet. Strange…can't find that either… Where do I enter my number of re-tweets in my profit and loss?…Has to be here somewhere…doesn't it?

Get the idea? None of that stuff matters. It's rubbish. It's just hot air spouted by people who don't know anything about business. The only thing that matters is how these things contribute to your bottom line, just like everything else you do. So then, how are your online strategies *creating business opportunities?* How is it you are building a website and social media platform that *attracts and connects with your target market?* How are you *creating a fusion* between the online and offline aspects of your business? How are you working towards being *effective* online and not just *popular?*

SHOW…ME…THE…MONEY.

EXERCISE: Getting social

1. Carefully consider your social media plan. How are you measuring whether it is successful or not? Do you know how many sales it generates? Are you using social media in a productive way that puts money in the bank, or are you just using it to 'stay in touch' or because you think you should be?

2. How much time and money are you spending on social media as a percentage of your marketing budget? Unless you are an online business, this should be less than 50%. If you don't know the answer, that's a problem as well!

The importance of syncing your business

These days we all know about syncing all sorts of gadgets, and your business is no different. If it's not in sync you will get substandard performance and ultimately you'll be headed for trouble.

Is your social media in sync with the rest of your business? If you focus too much on one side of your business and neglect the others you are in trouble. You need a balance. You can't just focus on online and you can't just focus on offline. But what about businesses like Amazon, I hear you ask. Surely they can just focus on online? No, they can't. Have a think about this simple issue: how long would Amazon stay in business if they regularly shipped the wrong products to their customers? Easy: not long at all. Managing their shipping is an offline function of their business.

The three legs that support your business are: physical, online and social media. If one of these isn't strong enough and in sync with the others, your business will fall over.

High tech and high touch

We're living in a world where the people element must always be present in your business, no matter what your high-tech approach is. Don't be a faceless company. Don't deal with your clients exclusively through your website or an automated phone service. Your clients don't want you to add to their problems, they want you to solve them.

The leverage offered by technology is great, but so is being human. Being 'high touch' means that as they work their way through your sales structure your customers have regular contact with a living and breathing human being. Give them a number they can call, and make sure it's answered by a person, not a machine. Give them the name of a customer concierge they can deal with, and make sure that person follows through on their transaction. There's nothing more annoying for customers than having to deal with a different person each time they contact your company.

To make sure you continue to be high touch as you grow, the people element of your business needs to be scalable. If we think about Brendan and his coffee shop, one of his unique selling propositions might be that he has the best barista in Melbourne. But is this scalable? Clearly not. It doesn't matter how good this guy is, he can't serve 20 customers at once. To deal with this, as he grows, Brendan then needs to find the second-best barista in Melbourne just *before* demand requires it, and then he needs to add another, and so on, staying just ahead of the demand from customers. As your business grows, the number of customer service staff, support staff, receptionists, call centre staff, and all of your other customer functions, need to grow with it just slightly ahead of demand.

The high touch aspect of your business is also about making an emotional connection. For Brendan, this could be baking muffins at the front of the store, so that the smell greets people as they walk in. Or if you are a mechanic, have a nice reception area with a coffee machine and a full-time receptionist to make clients feel welcome; don't make them walk into your greasy and grimy workshop.

EXTREME FOLLOW-UP PROCESS

To make sure you capitalise on every lead you generate, you need an **Extreme Follow-up** Process (EFU). We've already mentioned generating and following up leads, but now that we're getting into the nitty gritty of your business we're going to take this one step further.

An extreme follow-up process is making it non-negotiable that *every single lead you generate* is followed up, promptly and thoroughly. Every one. You can't go out of your way to create opportunities and then go to sleep when the leads come in. You need to be non-negotiable and demanding about following up current and future clients. You need to ensure that you are playing at your optimum best here. If your marketing, sales, customer retention and fulfilment strategies are not approached with extreme follow up, they will simply be expenses for your business and they will kill you.

I know a lot of people hate the 'sales side of things'. But let me give you the brutal truth: *there is no 'sales side of things'*. Sales is an integral part of any business; it's not optional. It's not something you can take or leave. If you are worried about being 'salesy', what on earth are you doing in business? You are trying to sell stuff, aren't you? I'm sure you didn't invest $300,000 of your own money so you could sit around in an empty store or quiet office because you didn't want to bother anybody. Let me define a business for you: it sells stuff and makes a profit. That's it. Selling.

If you think you are too quiet or too shy or don't have the 'right personality' to sell, you're completely and utterly wrong. You don't need to be as smart as Bill Gates or as charming as Hugh Jackman to be a great salesperson. Like anything in business this is something you can learn. This is something you *must* learn.

The other thing that holds people back is thinking they are a nuisance when they try to sell to people. That's just head trash. You have a great product or service. You know who needs it. You know why they need it. You know where they are. You can take them from frustration to freedom. How are you being a nuisance? If you sell the latest hip, rad, trendy skateboard outfits and you knock on the door of an old folks home, *that's* certainly being a nuisance, but that's not what you're doing, is it? You're going to approach your carefully defined target market with confidence and clarity.

The extreme follow-up process is a building block. It creates leverage. It's imperative that you don't have staff who are reluctant to contact people who say 'maybe'. You may be a small team but you can run a big business if you know who you are and what you do and everybody is on board. How can you not have a go? How can you not follow up in accordance with your culture and plans? Follow up *today*, not tomorrow, this morning, not this afternoon. Continue to show your clients you care and continue doing the right thing. If it's not okay they will tell you: they will go elsewhere. If you are watching your scoreboard you will know if it's working or not.

The extreme follow-up process is critical for making a profit. Your biggest result is to get money in via operating cashflow. You need to be in the business of making and growing money. At the end of the day we are all brothers and sisters in small business to something called profit; we've just chosen different ways to get there. Brendan makes coffee. I coach business owners. Maybe you're a plumber or an accountant or a builder or a lawyer. It doesn't matter; in the end we're all in it for the same thing.

If you do a great job creating an enquiry you must do a *better* job converting that enquiry into a customer. They need you. How can you not follow up!

WALKING THE TALK

If you're not giving your customers your best, why would they come back to you? You need to be the best you can be, and you also need to let your customers know that you are. Personally, I don't care about your experience or your education or your background, I just want to know that you're giving me your all. That's what will keep me coming back to your business. You must back up what you say and walk the talk. You must be congruent with – and just behind – your identity.

To help establish if you are walking the talk, let's have a look at the **Congruency Matrix**. I think the top 1% of business people succeed because they have the attributes shown in the table opposite. The key here is not just that they *appear* to have these attributes, but they actually *do possess them*. It's not about being slick and presenting a false front to the world in an attempt to attract business; it's about truly incorporating these things into your business, and then following through on them.

EXERCISE: Being, Doing and Having

Have a look at this table.

1. Circle or write down the ones you believe you personally are currently doing, and the ones you need to get better at. Then, for the ones you need to get better at, write down how you are going to do this.

2. Circle or write down the ones you believe your business is currently doing, and the ones your business needs to get better at. Then, for the ones your business needs to get better at, write down how you are going to do this.

The Congruency Matrix

BEING What is the DNA of you/your business?	DOING How do you/does your business behave?	HAVING What attributes do you/your business have?
• I value my worth and expertise. • I have clarity on the solutions I provide. • My intention and purpose is defined. • I am conscious. • I am visionary. • I am in growth mode. • I am brilliant at the basics. • I am an influencer of change. • I am a go-to expert in my field of expertise.	• I am disciplined. • I am an opportunist. • I am congruent. • I follow through. • I am a good, committed, solid communicator.	• I am an influencer. • I am an expert in my field. • I am connected. • I am leveraged. • I am an abundant influencer with the world. • I am living the quality of life I deserve. • I am profitable. • I am a leader of a champion team. • I am serving the clients I desire. • I am spending more time with my loved ones doing the things I love.

Then, if you are going to walk the talk, you must not only show your current and future clients that your business has these attributes, you must *follow through* with clarity and confidence.

Who are you? Where are your strengths? In what areas are you weak? You may need to get external help for your weaknesses, but to be attractive to your clients you need to show your strengths.

If you are going to walk your talk, that's how you need to be behind the scenes as well as in the open, and you need to do it with respect and humility. You've probably heard this before: you have the same number of hours in the day as Richard Branson (or Bill Gates or Janine Allis), so you can do what they do. This doesn't make any sense to me. Who *cares* what Richard or Bill or Janine do with their 24 hours? I sure don't. I only care what *I* do with *my* 24 hours. Worrying about anything else is a complete waste of time.

Do your best, all day, every day. What more can you expect of yourself?

 ## CHAPTER GEMS

- You measure your online success by how much money it puts in the bank. Nothing else.

- Being 'high touch' means that as they work their way through your sales structure your customers have regular contact with a living and breathing human being.

- To make sure you capitalise on every lead you generate, you need an Extreme Follow-up Process.

- You must back up what you say and walk the talk.

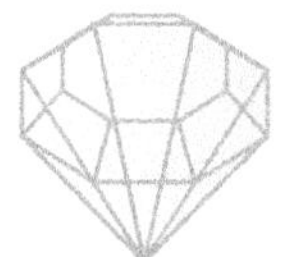

15. VICTIM VS VICTOR

One of my mentors, Brad Sugars, introduced me to this concept. Have a look at the diagram below.

Above and Below the Line

The diagram shows two different ways you and your staff can approach things. Above the line are the ingredients for success, below the line are the ingredients for failure. Unfortunately many businesses choose to operate below the line in an environment of blame and lack of trust, and with a victim mentality. Operating above the line requires more energy and effort, which is why many people stay below. But above the line is where you achieve victory.

Have a think about your business. Are you and your team members above or below the line? If the answer is above, you get a gold star. If the answer is below, you need to make some decisions about what you are going to do about that. And remember, you need brutal truth. You can pretend you are above the line if you like, but the only person you will be fooling is yourself, and that doesn't help you a whole lot.

MOVING ON UP

If you are currently operating below the line, how do you take yourself and your staff above? The answer I often hear to this question is *leadership*, but I think leadership is an overused term. Showing leadership is certainly important, but it doesn't magically solve all your problems. Getting from below the line to above is about *management*. It's about actively intervening to steer your ship in the right direction. Yes, doing this yourself and showing leadership is part of the process, but there's much more to it than that. It's about getting the culture right and the rules of the game right.

To find out how your business is travelling in this regard, score each person on your team as above or below the line – including you. Rank everybody as a +1 if you think they operate above the line or a –1 if they are below the line. You can rank them as +1 if you think they are below but are close to being above and you think you can get them there.

Once you decide on the culture that you are going to move

forward with you need to manage people from each stage to the next. Take them from denial to excuses to blame to responsibility to accountability to ownership. If you have staff who are operating at denial or excuses you can do your best to move them up if you think they can achieve this, but you might be better moving them out.

What is the percentage of your team that is above the line versus below the line? Now it's time to ask yourself a brutal truth question: how did they get there? Who led them there? The fish rots from the head down. If most of your staff are below the line, is it possible *you* are the problem?

So, what are you going to do about it? You cannot just lead people away from below the line, you need to manage them.

People in **denial** need to be given ultimatums. You're either going up or out. People who are in denial in your business will rot everything. If you are comfortable with staff being in denial it's either because you are lazy or you don't know how to get them out of this stage (and after reading this book you won't have that excuse any more).

How do you manage people into not giving **excuses**? Within your business, make it a habit to ask more *how* questions rather than *why* questions. *How* questions take you forward and solve problems, *why* questions leave you going nowhere and looking for somebody to blame. When something goes wrong, ask, 'How are we going to fix this so that it doesn't happen again?' That allows people to be proactive and take responsibility for solving the problem. Simply asking, 'Why did this happen?' is thoroughly unproductive. It doesn't actually solve the problem and it leaves people trying to point the finger at everybody else. If you ask more *how* rather than *why* questions, you will get solutions rather than excuses. This is also an area where it's imperative that you know your scoreboard. You'll have problems moving people out or up if you don't have the data for your business. You'll keep getting excuses from staff and you'll have no way to refute them because you don't have evidence.

How do you manage **blame**? A culture of pointing the finger is – sadly – common in many organisations. One of the keys to removing blame in a business is making sure you are creating rhythm in meetings where open and honest conversation is allowed. You need to be proactive to lead this so that your team members become reactive to the opportunity to be counted upon. Give them the opportunity to prove themselves. Challenge them. Let them take responsibility and give them the chance to rise to the occasion.

For your business to be effective all your staff need to be at least at the level of **responsible**. Have you provided an environment to give them the ability to respond? Are they responsible because somebody is looking over their shoulder (fear) or are they responsible of their own accord? Somebody who is only responsible when somebody else is watching is a potential de-selection. Somebody who takes responsibility themselves is a candidate for promotion.

Is it a push or pull system that you've created to hold people **accountable**? People in denial need a push, either up or out. What is the scoreboard that people can use to see what they are achieving? How are you going to move forward in accordance with your plan?

Ownership is about loyalty and growth. It's not something that's in your back pocket, it's in the heart and mind. When people in your business reach this stage they are just as committed and motivated as you are. They have bought into your vision and dreams and accepted them as their own.

Give your staff a plan and scoreboard and the opportunity to hit it out of the ball park. Create an environment where people have the opportunity to succeed, big time. To get the best results you need to hire people on attitude and you need to lead on attitude.

And what about you? Which one are you sitting on? Which would you *like* to be sitting on? What are you going to do about it?

Pinnacle Health Club is a great example of a business that has fully utilised these tactics. In an industry that is getting hammered, these guys are going toe to toe with the traditional big boys. How? They have put time and effort into their team, their vision, their mission and goals. They and their staff take ownership of these and are accountable for them. They have increased transparency and use of their scoreboard. They know they will fail occasionally but they will learn from this. Everybody in the business is responsible for their actions and what they believe in.

They now have four locations and generally don't lose clients in a market that's very competitive. And it's all to do with above and below the line. They own this and operate above the line, and it's contagious to their team.

Promotions, bonuses and de-selection

A great way to manage staff through this process is by making promotions probable and relevant. Give your staff something meaningful to aspire to and work with them to help them get there. Remember, the performance of your staff is critical to the success of your business, so do everything you can to help. The better they do the better you'll do.

Bonuses can also be useful, but they must be random bonuses. Paying a bonus at a clearly defined sales target will see staff focus on that target to the detriment of everything else. You don't want people obsessed with a number, you want them focused on doing their job as well as they can. A bank manager once told me about how ineffective their bonus system was. At the end of each year, the teller who signed up the most clients to new products received a huge bonus. One of his tellers took this to heart, and she offered every single customer new products on every transaction. If you went in to withdraw $20 she would try to sell you a mortgage. The manager didn't know what to do; how can you discourage this when your bonus system is the motivator? This teller won the bonus by a mile but she hadn't done her job well at all. I also know a book editor who once received a $7,000 bonus because one of his books went through the roof, but he'd edited this book to the best of his ability just the same as every other book he'd worked on. Sure he appreciated the money, but how does this encourage him to do a better job? These are great examples of how not to offer bonuses.

Also important is de-selection. Once you start laying down the new rules, give individuals the opportunity to say, 'I'm out of here. This culture and this environment is not for me.' If any of your staff members react like this then it's better for all concerned that they leave.

TRUST AND CREDIBILITY = WIN–WIN–WIN

I don't mean you need to get all emotional about your business; I mean you achieve win–win–win when everybody involved takes true ownership of what you do and how you do it. You'll be clear on where you're going and how you're going to get here. You'll talk the talk and walk the walk. There's no going back from that point.

Have a think about buying an engagement ring. It doesn't have to be a big rock. What matters is that you've made a decision and a commitment and that you follow through on it.

Every time you grow there will be a choke point. Having the trust of your people and your customers and the credibility that you will push through because you have in the past is paramount here. You need continual commitment to being high touch and high tech. Trust in business means correcting wrongs and always striving for what's right.

It's not about people trusting you personally but trusting your business because it has developed its own identity. If your business develops trust and credibility it's win–win–win. Your business wins because it goes from strength to strength. Your customers win because they get great outcomes. And your industry wins because you create new standards and benchmarks.

The plan is not as important as the *planning*. The process is more important than the final result. The process of looking closely at your business, of making tough decisions, of facing the brutal truth will take your business from deadwood to diamond. The size, carat and cut of the diamond that you become will also be dependent on the jeweller who creates it. That's why it's important to have a coach who has been there before. Your coach and your board of directors, and how you choose them, are crucial. That's why I started Board of Directors 12, to help people through this process (see page 241 for more information).

Remember: **Get brilliant at the basics.**

 ## CHAPTER GEMS

- Have a think about your business. Are you and your team members above or below the line?

- Once you decide on the culture that you are going to move forward with you need to manage people from each stage to the next.

- A great way to manage staff through this process is by making promotions probable and relevant.

- When you and your staff start operating from the heart, that's how you win.

CASE STUDY: MIA Consulting Services

MIA Consulting Services provides support to businesses wanting to increase their business opportunities with government, the Victorian government in particular. It delivers workshops, programs and consulting services aimed at improving the opportunities of a business to engage with government and to win government quotes and tenders. Let's find out more.

1. What problems were you facing in your business?

I always felt that the business could be successful but didn't know how to bridge the gap between delivering services only, to building a business. I didn't have the confidence to know how to build a business, and a highly successful business at that. In particular, I didn't understand the structure and systems required to build a business. Finally, I feared success in terms of the time and effort required to build a business.

2. Why do you think these problems occurred?

As a subject matter expert I had 100% confidence in the services I was delivering. However, with a strong public sector background I lacked the business acumen required to operate a business. Secondly, being so close to the content of the advice I was providing I didn't value it as an outsider would. I needed an independent viewpoint, coupled with an expert business perspective, to highlight that value to me.

3. What was holding you back?

Confidence and real knowledge that building a (successful) business wouldn't take time away from my young family was holding me back and to knowing what steps to take to build a business.

4. At what point did you recognise that you needed help, and what motivated you to get it?

This was when I realised that the business was stagnating. The business wasn't growing in terms of client base or service offerings. I also found myself providing services that I wasn't enjoying. The business and I both needed a change and I recognised Stefan as an opportunity to change.

5. What did you learn that helped you solve these problems?

Through Stefan I identified the business model that best suited both my personality type, and the core strengths of the business, and I began to make changes to support this business model. A key learning was to remove myself as CEO and focus on being the subject matter expert in delivering services, while someone else focused on being the CEO. This doesn't mean that I don't focus on the business it just means that it doesn't have to be an ongoing process which means that when I do focus on the business it's more fun than overwhelming.

6. What systems have you put in place that have helped your business?

We have introduced the following systems:

- Tracking key numbers such as leads, number of quotations and conversion rates
- Managing a default diary to support activities like client follow up, tender reviews for clients, and other activities to focus on working 'on' the business
- 'Work in progress' scheduling tools
- Managing the customer experience, including systematic customer follow-ups.

7. What was the biggest single change you made to yourself or your business that helped turn things around?

Stepping away from the CEO role and focusing on being the subject matter expert was my biggest change.

8. What other changes have you made and how have they helped?

All of these changes have better positioned the business in terms of increased service offering and increased customer base, but

have also injected a new level of enthusiasm and enjoyment into
the business:

- Incremental 90 day KPI planning – understanding key
  numbers and how the business is tracking against achieving
  them has been very powerful
- Introducing strategies to increase 'stickiness' of previous
  clients and potential clients
- Introduction of new workshop/program offering based on
  direct learnings from Stefan
- Development of a marketing plan that includes a social
  media strategy
- Embarking on strategic business relationships/partnerships.

9. What fears or challenges did you have to overcome? How did you do this?

The biggest fear was that of success, i.e. the fear that the more
successful you become the more time you are working on the
business. This was overcome progressively. Stefan has
constantly maintained that while business owners have to work
hard, it's not a 24x7 requirement – if a business acts smartly
and implements the right systems, and leverages people,
systems, finance, etc. Through my 10 month journey with
Stefan I can clearly understand how to work smart and manage
our time around our family. We don't work longer hours. My
husband and I enjoy quality time with our children and have the
satisfaction of watching the business grow.

10. What advice do you have for other small business owners who are currently struggling?

My advice is to know your numbers – however simple they are.
Prepare a simple 90 day plan with KPIs against key targets – for
example, number of new contracts, weekly revenue, number of
team meetings – and track progress against these. It's amazing
how motivating it is to track your progress against your own
numbers.

11. How is your business performing now? Has this exceeded your expectations?

In the time I have worked with Stefan the revenue base of the business has steadily increased and I have increased the range of services offered by the business. The business has grown from operating as a sole trader to a business that supports four professionals. The profile of the business has increased, including my profile as a government subject matter expert, and most importantly we're having fun with the business.

12. What non-monetary achievements have you achieved?

These include:

- An increase in reputation
- Enjoyment in the business
- Increased service offerings – including the 12 session workshop program
- Engagement of two sub-contractors to further build on the service offerings of the business.

13. What changes do you still need to make to your business, and why?

There are further systems required particularly around sales and customer management in our business. We also need better use of 'to achieve' versus 'to do' planning. I'd like to extend our business planning out from 12 months to 5 years and update internal systems, such as the leads and quotation register, and other systems to support tracking of key numbers.

14. Where do you think your business will be in five years time?

Our goals for five years time include:

- $2 million revenue per annum
- Minimum of five personnel
- Pre-eminent organisation for Victorian government knowledge
- Strategic partnerships (3 or 4) that support the continued

growth of the business – financially, and are positioned within the identified market.

15. If you hadn't made an effort to get help, where do you think you would be right now?

I would still be delivering services without having a sense of growing a business. I would be having many, many ideas for the business without a plan or idea of how to implement them. This would frustrate me and result in me losing the enjoyment I had in starting the business. My husband would still be an employee for a large corporate, looking for opportunities to move into the business.

16. How has turning your business around improved your life?

My husband has joined the business, which has immediately improved our quality of life. We are able to better manage our work load and spend more quality time with each other and our family. We are also building something that is rewarding, both financially and non-financially.

17. What big goal have you recently achieved in your business?

We have employed two sub-contractors.

18. What big goal have you recently achieved in your life?

We have taken a family holiday to our dream holiday island without having to worry about 'applying for leave', the financial situation, or what was waiting for us back at the office.

Part 5: Certification

> There is a spiritual aspect to our lives – when we give we receive – when a business does something good for somebody, that somebody feels good about them!
>
> —Ben Cohen, Ben & Jerry's

The future is very much a figment of our past.

Certification is not about what you do, it's about what others are saying about what you do. It's the culmination of all the effort and hard work you've put in. At this point somebody has rubber-stamped that you are a diamond. They are saying it works. It's approved. It ticks the boxes. This business delivered what it promised, and more. Certification is about people on the outside confirming all these things about your business. It's about independent arbiters assessing you and saying, 'It's a three carat diamond, and here's why'. Certification is about external influencers looking in.

The future is a component of your past and what you have set up. Determining what is the clarity, cut, colour and carat of your business will determine where it is today. These aspects are now coming to fruition. You're not ending up somewhere unexpected, because you created a plan and stuck to it. You didn't set out for London and land in Detroit.

This point is usually reached at the three to five year mark after you started to make and follow your strategic plan. And, because growing your business is a never-ending process, once you reach this point you will go back to mastery and start again.

If you continue to be in growth mode and operate at your Personal Best, what will your business look like in 20 years time? It's not so much the plan, it's the planning. Nothing more, nothing less. It's the depth of strategy. How is the market moving? How do you go with it? It's mastery at a new level. It's about reinventing yourself within the reputation that you've already created.

You need to ask: Where are we? Where could we be? What needs to be done?

The beaten track that you walk on now has nothing to do with the first step but everything to do with the most recent. It's not about who you're going to be but who you are right now. There are plenty of examples in history where reputation meant nothing when a company took a dive. If you start doing things incorrectly or start taking short-cuts, you will be punished.

It's almost at this point that the real work begins. How you sustain and build from the reputation you've created is critical.

16. RIGHT PEOPLE FOR RIGHT RESULTS

Having the right people is an absolute non-negotiable for your business to achieve certification. By now you've probably built your business to the point where you have 1, 2, 3 or 10 staff. If, at this stage, you have started to earn a great reputation, you are at the perfect point to start attracting the right people to take your business onwards and upwards. You will begin attracting people at a higher level and they will execute in accordance with your strategic plan for growth.

THE FIVE Rs

There are five key aspects to getting the people part of your business right. I call these the Five Rs. They are:

1. **Right people.** Not too hard to understand! You must have the right people. They must be aligned with your goals and your desired outcomes. They must be as

committed to the success of your business as you are. If you don't have the right people, the remaining four Rs won't help you.

2. **Clear about Roles.** Clearly defining the roles of everybody in the business is imperative. Without a clearly defined role, how can you expect to get the best out of somebody? How will they know what they should be doing? How will you judge whether they are succeeding or failing? How will they know what their position is in the organisation?

3. **Clear about Responsibilities.** Clarity about responsibilities is also crucial. Without it you'll end up with an inefficient workforce that doesn't know who is supposed to do what. And without clear responsibilities there can be no accountability.

4. **Getting paid the Right money.** This is a no-brainer. Treat your staff as an *investment*, not a cost. The right people will return your investment many times over. Paying the right money will help you attract and retain the right people, and your business will reap the rewards.

5. **Providing the Right results.** This is about congruency. If you've just designed a great widget, that doesn't really help my business if I wanted you to design a doodad. Everything your people do must be in line with your long-term strategic plan.

Of the Five Rs, most businesses have problems paying the right money. Business owners think low salaries are a great way to cut costs, and then they scratch their heads wondering why they don't get the right results. Your ability to attract and retain the best staff will be highly compromised if you don't pay the right money. You don't have to go overboard, but you do have to pay staff salaries that reflect their value to the business. If you don't, one of your competitors will, and that's how you lose the best people. Keep in mind that your best staff are always the ones with the most options, so you must pay them what they deserve to keep them.

As my mentor once said, 50% of something successful is way better than 100% of something that's not, so one great person can replace two or three good or average people.

EXERCISE: The five Rs

Write down the five Rs on a piece of paper, and then write a few sentences about how your business performs in each area. In which areas are you doing well? What areas need to be improved? How will you make these improvements?

1. Right people.

    ____

2. Clear about Roles.

    ____

3. Clear about Responsibilities.

    ____

4. Getting paid the Right money.

    ____

5. Providing the Right results.

    ____

TRAINING AND DEVELOPMENT

If you want to keep your staff, investing in their training and development is non-negotiable. Good salaries and a good reputation might attract them, but they won't keep them. By definition, the people you want to hire will be curious, bright and hard-working. How long do you think people like this will stay if you stick them in a corner and forget about them? You must invest in their training. I suggest a minimum of about 120 hours per annum of appropriate training for each staff member. Once again, consider it an investment, not a cost. The money you spend on the right training for the right people will more than pay for itself.

Here's a simple formula for you to keep in mind:

Fewer people + Paid more + Right training and development = HR success

Business owners are sometimes concerned that if they train their staff *too* well they will leave, wasting the time and money invested in them. If you think the only possible outcomes are train them and they leave versus don't train them and they stay, you can't win. You either create good staff who go elsewhere or keep staff and watch them stagnate.

But there is a third possible outcome: you train them well *and* they stay. If you do the right thing and look after your staff, you won't have to worry about them leaving. Create the right environment. Challenge them. Train them. Pay them well. Give them responsibilities and opportunities for growth and advancement. You won't even have to have the conversation. I know well-run businesses that have had staff members stay for 20 years. This used to be the norm but it is just about unheard of these days. Make this long-term staff retention a goal of your business. Training and development increases both performance and loyalty.

BUILDING FOR THE FUTURE

You're not building for today, you're building for the future. With this in mind, you must ask yourself the following two questions about each member of your staff:

* Would you enthusiastically re-hire that person if you had the opportunity?

* Do you think that person has the potential to be the best person in their position in three to five years from now? Think about where your business will be in three to five years. Does that person fit your plan? Will they be the best person at exactly what you need them to be doing? You can't get to where you're going in three to five years and then have to start building again because you didn't arrive with the right people.

If you answered *no* to either of these questions, you have to think long and hard about why that person is still with you. I regularly see business owners struggle with making decisions about removing staff. Too often workers are left in place because the boss can't find the courage to get rid of them, or they think they'll get better despite all evidence to the contrary, or they are just not sure they can find somebody else better.

The people you have coming with you are critical. You don't have room for passengers. At the moment you might still be playing B-grade and that's fine, as long as your people have the capacity to play A-grade when you get to that level. A-grade players playing a B-grade game are better than B-grade players trying to play an A-grade game. You need to help your people go up or de-select themselves.

Hiring great people is a numbers game. A business that has established a solid reputation will attract the best. It's a magnet. Ask yourself, did you get a lot of A-grade people applying for the last position you advertised? When hiring, you need to make sure you are truly selling the business and its vision. You need to sell the business to potential employees with the same vigour that you use to attract potential clients in target markets.

GOOD PEOPLE AT EVERY STEP

There may be lots of different people involved in your business at all different levels, and you have control over all of them. With the plans you put in place and the way you run your business you can make sure you attract the right people at every level. As we've discussed, your business really has four customers, and for continued growth you need to look after them all:

- **Business owner (most likely you):** Demands profits. That's what the business is for, right?
- **Team:** Need to know they are going somewhere so they can buy in. They need to be looked after, to feel valued. They need training, opportunities and their wages paid on time. They need to be part of something that is growing, not dying.
- **Suppliers:** They are backing you to grow so that you keep on buying more from them. Great suppliers bring much value to your business.
- **Customers:** These are the people who hand over their hard-earned folding stuff. Without them you have no business, full stop. They are backing you for delivery of a product or service that they need. They are counting

on you to take them from frustration to freedom, and they will continue to back you as long as you do.

Don't wait for 'one day' to get on top of your people issues. One day is now. You can sort this out NOW.

 ## CHAPTER GEMS

- There are five key aspects to getting the people part of your business right: the Right people, who are clear about Roles, clear about Responsibilities, getting paid the Right money, and providing the Right results.

- If you want to keep your staff, investing in their training and development is non-negotiable.

- With the plans you put in place and the way you run your business you can make sure you attract the right people at every level.

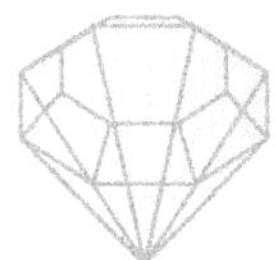

17. WHAT ARE THEY SAYING ABOUT YOU?

REPUTATION

Reputation is about being attractive to the four key stake-holders: the owners, the team, suppliers and customers.

Having a good reputation means that you are getting rubber-stamps from people in each of these categories. These rubber-stamps are the coming of age for your business. It means that your business is recognised as being worthy of providing an opportunity. It's maturing. It is known for attracting good people. Better suppliers are non-negotiable, and A-grade suppliers are turning up. At this stage, your business might be winning awards, and you should start to be recognised as a top 10 industry benchmark, either locally or globally. Your financial position is robust and you are achieving steady profits. You are attracting more and better opportunities. Your products and services are reaching a level of innovation, maturity and breakthrough. You deliver on results. You are growing steadily and with focus. As far as results achieved, you have testimonials and case studies. You know how to be personal but still in touch with technology and innovation.

A good reputation is a combination of all this, and more. It's not easy to pin down and there's no way to put a dollar figure on it, but I can safely say that without a good reputation your business is closer to being deadwood than a diamond.

VALIDATION

There are a number of ways your business can achieve validation.

Awards are a great acknowledgement that you have achieved a level of excellence. These can be awards within your industry and also general business awards. They can be local, national or global. And it's not just about winning. It's about putting your hand up because you're backing yourself. It's about staying focused on the one critical thing that makes you who you are and being recognised for that.

Recognition from your industry and the media is also a form of validation. How is it you are perceived and sought after in your industry? Are you being asked to speak? Are you asked to comment in the media on particular aspects of your industry? This means you are now being recognised for what you do. I've been interviewed in the media many times before, and I wasn't speaking about synchronised swimming! I get called to comment on small and medium business and profits, because that's what I'm known for and that's what I do. That's the validation I receive.

RAVING FANS

You know you have achieved deep target market penetration when people are starting to wear your lapel buttons because they are proud to do so. It's not just that they are talking about you – they *belong*. They are genuinely part of your tribe. They believe in you. This is true customer loyalty that has developed from your customer delight culture. This is certification.

You don't need to be a $10 million business to achieve this. In the early days, having raving fans can be a personal relationship. At this point they are fans for you but not your business. You have got through the initial growth phase and placed your stake in the ground, but work still needs to be done. Right now you might only have five raving fans. That's fine. Even five raving fans is valuable certification. That's something for you to build on. As you grow you will develop more levels of raving fans and they will help you get through choke points.

Don't think small. Think big! Are you ready to put your hand up? Are you ready to enter your industry awards? It puts you out there to be counted and to get feedback. The process of aiming for it is valuable in itself. Don't worry about winning. It's like leadflow and workflow; if you aim to grow it the benefits will flow.

All of the case studies in this book are thriving examples of these three areas. They have loyal, repeat customers. They are go-to organisations. Their message is clear and they are not confusing the market. Existing clients are bringing new clients. They have active referral programs, and you can't do this without a reputation for providing solutions.

Be clear about where you are building your reputation. These businesses are.

 ## CHAPTER GEMS

- Reputation is about being attractive to the four key stakeholders: the owners, the team, suppliers and customers.

- Recognition from your industry and the media means you are being recognised for what you do.

- You know you have achieved deep target market penetration when people are starting to wear your lapel buttons because they are proud to do so.

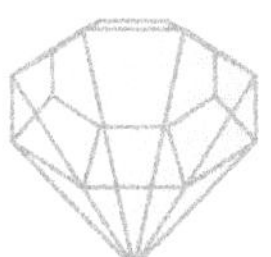

18. WHERE ARE YOU NOW?

MONEY MASTERY

Business is a bit more serious now; it's no longer *I'll just wake up and have a crack*. You're building momentum with persistence and follow through, and each and every day you execute, execute, execute. Finance is no longer a poor and ignored cousin. Your operating cashflow projection is truly relevant to your planning and decision-making. Looking at the profit and loss is not a sin. You know what your breakeven is, inclusive of profit. It is both established and achieved. You know this because you understand and carefully watch the scoreboard every week, month and quarter. Your ratio analysis for different areas is advanced. Balance sheets are studied and trends recognised and understood. As we've already examined, the three key scoreboards you need to thoroughly understand are profit and loss, the balance sheet and the cashflow forecast.

Understating ratio analysis and the trends of business will put you in a strategic position to be asking the right questions and confirming the data which ultimately leads to better results. Show me your activity and I'll share with you with precision what your outcomes will be. This is the level of mastery you need to reach too.

SO THAT'S THE BRUTAL TRUTH

At this stage brutal truth is what got you here. We discussed it right up front. Getting the right cut and colour is dependent on brutal truth. You must be open and honest and seek 360 degree feedback. Brutal truth must be a central aspect of the culture of your business.

You must take every opportunity to be proactive and follow through. You must see the trends coming and not wait for them to appear. Waiting to see if something just turns up is not okay. You must get out there and make it happen, and act immediately when opportunities appear.

Having very clear indicators is what a good feedback system is all about. You need the brutal truth from everybody you deal with. You need to know where you are performing well and where you need more work. You need to be okay with feedback that says you're rubbish. Getting poor feedback is not a problem; what matters is how you deal with it. You must have the ability to say sorry when something has gone wrong. Don't beat yourself up; just fix it. Nobody expects you to be perfect, but they certainly do expect you to handle things quickly and with humility when things go wrong.

Conduct exit interviews with team members, suppliers and customers. Find out why they are going. Don't get mad or upset. Keep in mind that if good people are leaving it's partly your fault because you didn't create the right environment to keep them. Gain as much intelligence as you can to help stop good people leaving in the future. If certain staff members need to be let go that's also about brutal truth. You can't be scared about hurting feelings or getting negative feedback. That's rubbish. It's not personal. It's business.

The brutal truth has taken you from cut to carat. Now that you are at certification, it should be part of the underlying foundation of the culture of your business, and you can't let go of this now.

DON'T BREAK THE LAWS

There are three key laws in business and as with all laws they must not be broken.

Law of Attraction

The Law of Attraction states that by focusing on positive thoughts you can bring about positive results. It's an idea promoted by Michael Losier in his book called – wait for it – *Law of Attraction.*

So what's the deal? The Law of Attraction is about putting it out there and then talking the walk and walking the talk. It's about not having limiting beliefs or views on what's possible. It's 'I can', 'I will', 'I know' this will happen. It's about dare to dream. The Law of Attraction says that if you do this it will help you achieve your goals, but if you have negative thoughts then negativity is what you'll attract.

This is where you need focus, vision and alignment. We all

know people who get fired up about things and then go home and flop on the couch and watch re-runs of *Lost*. That's not going to get you to your dreams.

Law of Vacuum

The Law of Vacuum is about opening up and creating space for growth. If you're trying to attract something new into your life you have to make sure there is room for it. You have to plan in advance. You have to open up and create space. If you don't plan ahead for the growth and success of your business you won't have the capacity to handle it when it arrives, and that's worse than not achieving the growth at all because you'll create a lot of unhappy customers when you let them down.

Don't wait until the 11th hour. Don't wait until two minutes before the choke point to create something that's ready for growth. Open it up to suck it in. Plan in advance. Create space in your office, store or warehouse. Buy market share. Know what's coming around the corner and be ready for it.

Law of Reciprocity

The more you give the more you get. The more you provide positive result for others the more the world provides better results for you. It's about having an abundance mindset versus a scarcity mindset. It's about believing there's enough for everybody.

There will be people you serve who you have an inner instinct might rip you off. And they will. It will happen. But it's not your role to be the judge of what happens to them. You must believe in your intention: if you keep giving enough good to others good will come back to you.

One of my goals is to help 50 people become unencumbered millionaires by 2018. If I do that, is it only fair that the world gives me just some of that back? If I help people put food on their table isn't it okay for some of that to come back to me? Of course it is.

There's more than enough for us all, so don't be afraid of giving too much away.

Not-for-profits are competing with so many other organisations for the charity dollar. Success depends on how they make themselves attractive and the most appropriate for the clients they want to attract.

It's not just about receiving, it's about giving. I think this is one area where most businesses have to get better. They need to get better at helping people where they need to be helped. If people are helping me it's only fair and reasonable to help them back. It's not just a badge for your business, you have to go above and beyond. It's about having an abundance mindset rather than a scarcity mindset.

 ## CHAPTER GEMS

- Brutal truth must be a central aspect of the culture of your business.
- The Law of Attraction states that by focusing on positive thoughts you can bring about positive results.
- The Law of Vacuum is about opening up and creating space for growth.
- The more you provide positive results for others the more the world provides better results for you.

19. YOUR PERSONAL VALUES HIERARCHY

Just like your business, your personal values need validation and certification. If you haven't clearly articulated your personal values, how will you know if they are being achieved? How will you get the most out of life if you don't know what's important to you?

THE VALUES HIERARCHY

For me this certification comes from the **Values Hierarchy**. I know with clarity what my values are and how they fit into my life, and this allows me to assess whether I am living according to what truly matters to me. This hierarchy drives everything I do, every day. I don't usually share these values but it's important and I thought it would be beneficial, so here it is:

1. **Health:** If I'm not looking after myself, nothing else happens and I can't be who I need to be for my family.

If I can't get out of bed in the morning, if I take three or four sick days every month, none of my goals will be achieved. This is why health is number 1 on the list, even ahead of family. I need to be healthy to be there and provide for my family.

2. **Family:** I have two boys and a wife who I am extremely devoted to. Being a father and a husband are the most important jobs I do. I see it as my responsibility to provide security for my family, which motivates me in my business.

3. **Money:** This could also be 'business', because really it's the same thing. Some people don't like to say they value money – I've never understood that. I value money, a lot. I value money because if I have it I can provide for and look after my family. If I have money I can spend time with them and experience everything life has to offer. I like to think of money as a river that flows. We all have the opportunity to walk up to the river and grab as much as we can, or we can create a way to go to the river with buckets. Leaving a legacy for my family is also about money. It's also important to be authentic, credible and trustworthy, and live with integrity first. It's no good getting to the top but having blood on your shoes. Disagreements are okay and are part of the game, but you need to deal with problems with honesty and integrity. Don't burn bridges because you may need to cross them again later.

4. **Philanthropy:** This doesn't happen without the first three. That's why it's a hierarchy – the order matters. It might sound good to put philanthropy first, but if that's my priority ahead of money I won't have anything to be philanthropic with! As money grows,

philanthropy grows. It doesn't have to be millions of dollars. I don't want my name on an orphanage, I just want to help.

5. **Gratitude:** This is about going out of your way to say a genuine thanks to those who deserve it. It's about going out of your way to surprise. Greed leads to an ungrateful life, but there's nothing wrong with a desire for more if it's done in the right spirit. I make it a point to say five genuine thank-yous every day.

I teach this hierarchy to all my clients. You can copy mine if you like or come up with your own. It doesn't matter what it is, as long as it's right for you. I can teach you to make more money than you've ever had, but without this Values Hierarchy you have no rock to build on.

EXERCISE: Values

Have a think about your values hierarchy and what's important to you. See if you can create a list that represents your hierarchy of values. Once you do that, get in front of the mirror and read it out and link it all together.

Philanthropy and the giving back purpose

We all have a personal opinion on donating money. For some people philanthropy is their prime purpose, for others not so much. And that's okay. You can't judge other people on what they do. Like everything in your business, you should spend your time concentrating on your own decisions, not what others are doing. It's not about who has the biggest and deepest wallet. If you allocate a percentage of your profits to your philanthropic endeavours, the more you succeed the more you will be giving.

An aim for me is to be able to help disadvantaged kids around the world to learn the skills and tools of making money and being successful. I don't want to give them one meal; instead I want them to learn how to create thriving communities on the basis of business and then they can feed themselves on an ongoing basis. This is one of my dreams and one of my goals. It gives me purpose and is a key driver in everything I do. At some point I want to be able to take six months off every year so I can do this, and I truly believe I'm well on the way to reaching this goal.

I believe your business and your life will be better aligned if you have a greater purpose. I love meeting people who have achieved this in their lives. They have an aura around them. They know they are contributing and making a difference. I know people who are helping to build orphanages, assisting homeless people, working with animals, looking after the sick – the list of ways you can help is endless.

Do whatever you are comfortable with. Don't feel you have to compete with anybody else or make a song and dance about being a philanthropist. Just because you have reached the point of certification you don't necessarily have to give more. If you are giving away a percentage of your profits the dollar amount you are giving will go up anyway as you grow.

 ## CHAPTER GEMS

- You can have more money than you've ever had before, but without a Values Hierarchy you have no rock to build on.

- You should spend your time concentrating on your own decisions, not what others are doing.

- Your business and your life will be better aligned if you have a greater purpose.

SO, NOW WHAT?

Now, rest and relaxation! By the time you reach this point you get to sit back on the beach in Fiji and manage your business by phone. Your wonderful staff will keep the profits coming in, the systems you have built will purr along in your absence, and you just have to sit back and count your money.

Right? Surely that's what happens now?

Sorry, but if that's what you were expecting then you haven't been paying attention. It's brutal truth time again. Your reward for getting this far is you get to go back and do it all again. You see, you haven't arrived, this is just another stop along the way. In fact, there really is no end to this process. There isn't a business in the whole world that is perfect, that doesn't have room to grow or improve. The day you stop growing is the day you start dying.

Think back to the Quality of Life Ladder. You can always gain more knowledge, have bigger dreams, ask more questions, make better decisions, take more action, get better results and end up with an even better quality of life. There is absolutely no limit to how many times you can do this. Once you've taken your business from deadwood to diamond, you can take your business through another phase of growth and refinement and it will come out even stronger again at the other end. And then you can do it again, and again, and again, and… After every choke point you will go back to the start and go through this process again.

I want you to think long and hard about everything you've read in this book. Do you remember that bit where I said running a business is easy and after only a few years you'll be filthy rich and never have to work again? No, you don't, because it's not in here. You know that's not how it works.

So, why are you sitting around here? Get to it. Now. Right now! Remember your goal is to be bored and rich rather than excitable and broke. Just keep doing the things that work and get bored. Dare to dream. And what allows you to reach your dreams is this thing called profit. If you are not making profits by running your business lean and utilising your resources at their best and highest level, you will not be making profits to realise dreams, which ultimately means you will stop dreaming, which means your short-term fix is being excitable and broke.

Remember: **Get brilliant at the basics.**

CASE STUDY: Five Star Locksmiths

Five Star Locksmiths is a domestic, commercial, and industrial locksmiths specialising in restricted master key systems. The owner had spent a year building up his business after he had been in dire financial straits having lost his house, cars, almost everything he owned. Now, a year into his business, he had debt-collectors chasing him for unpaid debts and wanting to close his business down. This is when he contacted Stefan.

1. Why do you think these problems occurred?

They were a consequence of my previous bad debts and some unforeseen circumstances.

2. What was holding you back?

I lacked two things: money and knowledge.

3. At what point did you recognise that you needed help, and what motivated you to get it?

I couldn't run and hide from the debt collection agencies anymore and I heard one of my competitors who was doing quite well at the time mention something about business coaches. I thought maybe that's why he was so successful. I went and spoke to three or four business coaches. They wanted to charge me a small fortune to write me up a business plan, then, when I had more money they could help me more closely. This was not how I would learn more about business and get myself out of the situation that I was in. I then found my secret weapon!!! Stefan Kazakis. I had no idea how to deal with these people and I had no money to pay them as it was all tied up in my new little micro business. Stefan helped me negotiate my debt to nearly half of what it was. We fixed my cashflow issues and then started on the path to success.

4. What did you learn that helped you solve these problems?

I learnt the art of negotiation and how to start to manage my cashflow.

5. What systems have you put in place that have helped your business?

I don't know where to start. Here are a few:

- Cashflow management
- How and where to advertise
- How to monitor our advertising
- How to work out our conversion-per-lead-generated.
- Short- and long-term budgets and goals
- How to set up sales targets and manage new potential clients
- Implementing phone scripts
- Implementing a guarantee that increased my sales by 30%.

6. What was the biggest single change you made to yourself or your business that helped turn things around?

I found direction, motivation and confidence and was made accountable to my KPIs. I also had a greater understanding of the importance of numbers. I had to stop thinking like a locksmith and start thinking like a businessman.

7. What advice do you have for other small business owners who are currently struggling?

If you want to be successful, like a top athlete, look at your structures.

Sportspeople have dieticians, strength and fitness coaches, mentors, motivational speakers, short-term and long-term planned goals and people monitoring their progress.

If you want to succeed in business you need smart people around you. Like a great accountant and book-keeper and the best business coach in town (STEFAN KAZAKIS). Stefan can give you the equivalent guidance and support but in the world of business and finance, rather than sport.

8. How is your business performing now? Has this exceeded your expectations?

I couldn't be happier as we have nearly doubled our turnover every year since we started our journey together with Stefan. I pass on the knowledge that I have learned to my children so they understand the language and concepts of business and have an easier path to wealth than I did.

9. What specific goals, in dollar terms, have you achieved from implementing the changes you have made?

We have nearly doubled our turnover every year! I have more family time now than ever before and I have travelled more frequently for business and pleasure. I also have cash in my bank like never before!

10. What specific non-monetary achievements have you gained?

I feel that Stefan's knowledge and calmness and his clear way of thinking has flowed through to me and also my family. I have grown as a person and as a businessman and I hope in time to be able to be in a position to help others in the world less fortunate than myself and pass on the good karma that comes with smart and constant focused work.

11. What changes do you still need to make to your business, and why?

Business is an ever-changing world. I don't think you ever really get to the end. As soon as you think you have got it right there is always a better way of doing it. We are still very early on our journey with Stefan but look forward to growing our business bigger and more profitably, year after year.

12. Where do you think your business will be in five years time?

I believe deep in my heart that I will be a leader in my industry and will have a very successful business with a great structure and will have expanded our business into other states and maybe countries.

13. If you hadn't made an effort to get help, where do you think you would be right now?

I would be more than likely bankrupt and divorced and working on wages, unhappy with my life.

I was told I would never succeed because I was a fool. Some of my friends and family tried to discourage me from starting my own business because it was too hard and it was not for someone like me. I wanted to succeed for my family and to lead by example and to show them that they can achieve what they want out of life if they are prepared to do whatever it takes and not to listen to the noise. (The noise I refer to is the negative chatter from others and sometimes ourselves.)

14. What are your top five tips for other business owners?

- Get a business coach.
- Get a business coach.
- Get a business coach.
- Get a business coach.
- Get a business coach.

15. How has turning your business around improved your life?

I have financial direction for my family. I am calmer and clearer than ever before. My children have benefitted and will continue to benefit more financially than they previously would have. We have travelled more often and to exotic locations.

FINAL THOUGHTS

No matter how tough things are, if you want to reach your dreams you're just going to have to push through, regardless of what your circumstances are. You need deep-seated belief to make all of this happen, not only in your business but most importantly in your life. Business is not easy, but that doesn't mean it has to be hard. Regardless of what happens, and where you go with your business, you must have a 'whatever it takes' approach. Particularly in small business, hard work and consistent advancement in strategy are key to ongoing, predictable, strategic growth that will eventually earn you the key to the vault of your dreams.

What is important to you? Don't let anybody else decide this for you. Don't let anybody else hijack your dream or your vision. You may feel trapped and dissatisfied in your business right now, but that doesn't mean you need to walk away. When you get into business, be aware that there will always be choke points along the way, so you are going to have to keep returning to the start of the process and going through it again to get you through the next choke point and on to further growth. You'll have to start thinking about clarity again, and then cut, thinking about the size and structure of the business as you grow… and so on.

You must have the stamina to keep going and the fortitude to believe that what you are doing is making a significant difference to the people you have chosen to serve. It's about getting the accreditation and the certification from these people.

In the middle of all this it's important to have those moments of celebration and gratitude for the things you have – too often people wait for what they see as an extraordinary event to occur before they stop and look around and think about their lives.

Don't take things for granted. When things are going well, don't take your foot off the pedal; you must keep on going. Approach the next deal as if it's your most important, approach your next hire as though your business depended on it – from your first staff member to your one-thousandth. They are the custodians of what you are trying to build.

No matter where you are and what you do, surround yourself with people who are smarter than you. Surround yourself with people who are dream-makers, not dream-takers. And, as I have always done and still do, have a professional mentor on your side. It's not for everyone, but it *is* for those who truly want to go to the next level … and the next level after that, and so on … It's no different to professional sportspeople or musicians or professional anything – you need an outsider to take you across that gap from where you are now to where you want to be. If you want to hit it out of the park, you need somebody to make sure you are hitting it right.

Your frustrations will remain if you keep focusing on the problems and not how to solve them. Every single frustration that you have right now has a solution, as long as you allow yourself to look more widely beyond the problem. When all else fails, look in the mirror and go back to the formula for transformation that we examined at the start of this book. When all else fails, you must understand that there is only one individual in the way of something better than where you are now, and that's you.

I guarantee you can get past your current frustrations to achieve your big outcome if you commit to making the effort, and at the end of that road will be a stronger business and a better life.

Once again I would like to express gratitude to all my mentors, in particular to Mum and Dad, and to Basil, Brad and Keith. Your contribution has been profound. Thank you.

WHERE DO YOU WANT YOUR BUSINESS TO TAKE YOU?

YOUR PROFIT BLUEPRINT PLANNING SERIES

Business planning is so crucial to success but finding the time and expertise can be difficult. That's why we created the Your Profit Blueprint Planning Series.

This package gives you 4 × intensive strategic planning workshops in a 12-month period.

By attending the Your Profit Blueprint Planning Series you get the tools to develop a business plan that you can start implementing immediately.

It is a great choice for business owners who just need an injection of business planning strategy and new tools to keep them on the right path to profits and growth.

Each session lasts five hours. Attending Your Profit Blueprint is how a lot of businesses kick start their business growth. We don't believe in quick fixes or instant success here at Stefan Kazakis. Real success is a long-term game that takes continuous investment and improvement.

You will learn:

- Strategies to profit success unique to your business
- Problems that have been holding you back – and the solutions!
- The key way to differentiate your business
- Top reasons most growth plans fail
- The secret to high potential growth!

BUSINESS FUNDAMENTALS WORKSHOP SERIES

Get onto these Business Fundamentals Workshops that are helping small businesses create a road map to fast growth and sustainable profits. They are perfect for small business owners who lack the time or resources for one-on-one business coaching and, in fact, they offer a whole lot more as they're structured to target the three fundamental areas every business needs to get right and continuously improve in. Each module is a full-day training session.

The Business Fundamentals Workshop Series will help you create the underlying structure to build a business that is focused on being predictable for profit. The Workshop Series includes:

- **Operations Fundamentals**
  A vital workshop for every small business owner that is focused on all operational elements of business from daily predictable systems through to time management and execution and utilisation of all your resources. It's about learning the systems for creating systems.

- **Finance Fundamentals**
  The ultimate workshop to guarantee you are focused on the importance of understanding your financials.

This is the key to knowing where your cash comes from and goes to…and how to keep some of it. You'll learn how to read your financial statements, about the cashflow cycle and how to budget for profit within your breakeven.

- **Marketing Fundamentals**
A workshop designed to extract your uniqueness and discover what sets you apart from your competitors, plus learn how to use this to get more of the customers you want. You will also learn how to put together great campaigns with low acquisition cost and high lifetime value to your business growth.

- **Sales Fundamentals**
The definitive workshop to learn about the different types of salespeople and the difference between old selling and new. Sales is the only thing that puts money in your business, everything else takes it out, so you will learn to understand the question funnel and how to handle objections to gain better conversion rates in your business.

- **Customer Loyalty Fundamentals**
This workshop is about client fulfilment. Now you have done all the hard work to get them. You will learn about developing customer loyalty so that your customers keep coming back…time after time!

- **Team Fundamentals**
This workshop is all about building the dream team you've always wanted. Learn how to become a great leader and how to inspire them each and every day. Learn how to recruit great people and lead them to a business that works without you.

- **PLUS Power Negotiations 1–2–1**
  This full day workshop is designed for every possible negotiation that you and your business will face. Stefan will share with you the skills and the tools that the pros work with in terms of negotiating everyday and once-in-a-life-time deals. This workshop will equip you for all future negotiations and is an exclusive bonus to those enrolled in the Business Fundamentals Workshop Series.

BOARD OF DIRECTORS 12

This program is unique to Stefan Kazakis, and it's helping small businesses achieve incredible things, from huge increases in profits to building A-grade teams and attracting A-grade clients to putting the structures in place for long-term sustainable growth.

What is the Board of Directors 12 and how does it work?

Board of Directors 12 is a carefully structured business program that runs over four years in 12-month increments. You apply to join and will then be put in a group with up to 12 non-competing businesses. The group meets once a fortnight and each session is structured around strategic personal development and the importance to ensure the business owner or leader is positioning their business for sustainable double-digit profit growth.

The ultimate aim of this program is, within four years, to deliver an appropriate exit strategy for the owner, if that is what they wish for.

This program guarantees a transformation to a better quality of life.

PRIVATE ONE-ON-ONE COACHING

Business owners and management teams who require one-on-one strategy coaching can work with Stefan Kazakis. Private coaching takes many forms, ranging from fortnightly to weekly meetings, to half or full days, to three-day retreats focusing on strategic alignment of your business and management teams. General length of assignments are between 6 and 24 months.

INDEX

READ WHAT THEY SAY ABOUT STEFAN KAZAKIS

Stefan is the whole package – highly motivating, he keeps you accountable and teaches you the formula to running a successful business. He truly delivers more value than he ever promised. Time and time again I am blown away by his commitment to clients and the support he provides. Stefan teaches from experience. He is a coach who has lived, breathed and walked his talk. I would recommend Stefan to anyone who wants to develop a profitable business.

—**Jenny Boymal, Director, Jena Dyco International**

I knew my business needed some direction and a friend introduced me to Stefan. I enrolled in his Board of Directors 12 program and, to be honest, I'm not sure I would still be here if I hadn't. The constant support and direction have been invaluable to me, and my business has grown as a consequence. I totally recommend him as a person and a business coach.

—**Vicki Bentley, Bentley Interiors**

Twelve months ago, when I first met Stefan, I had been in business in excess of 25 years and was 59 years of age. Due to a number of factors, I was at my lowest ebb in business and in life in general. Repeat business had always kept us busy, however, due to number of our past clients now not in business and other varying factors, work flow had dried up completely. At Board of Directors 12, Stefan instilled confidence, and gave me focus to turn my business work flow – and therefore cash flow – around in a very positive way. I recommend Stefan to those who want to see their own input improve their team and business.

—**Ian Bennett, Corporate Design Pty Ltd**

Thanks for your help this year – it has been phenomenal. We didn't quite know what to expect when we came on board almost 10 months ago and now the results speak for themselves. It's been quite a journey and we couldn't have done it without you. You've been integral to our ongoing path to success. I'm looking forward to catching up in the New Year, and consolidating what we have learnt this year and implementing those things that you have been teaching us.

—**Doug Graham, Tough Glass Worx**

We have increased our average dollar sale from $250 to $369 – that's a 67% increase.

—**Clint Sharp, Pinewood Automotives**

A $175k bottom line profit would make it almost a $100k increase within the 12 months.

—**David Haspell, Signarama**

Over the last few years the continued 'belief and push' by you for me, to take the next step of not only being a business owner but a true leader, has continued to pay big time. My ability to share The Drain Man's common goals with my team, and the commitment to create an environment in our organisation where you are either promotable or deselected, has put us in good stead as we strive to set the benchmark in our industry. Our people and culture growth has been strategic and measured. Our business growth is due to striving towards a personal best and everyone serving our clients as VIPs. I'm truly proud of the outcomes to-date and the possibility of higher levels in the future. Gratitude to you and all that you do for me and my entire team.

—**Brendan Dover, The Drain Man**

We have improved our profit from a negative $190k to being on target for a $200k plus profit this year. Since I started on the program I have decreased my debt which was accumulated over five years from $230k to almost paid off.

—**Richard Dover, Taste Tempters**

Without the support and guidance from Stefan and the Board of Directors 12 Program, I would never have won a $75,000 contract (from 800 applicants Australia-wide). Stefan got me to believe in myself. Now, I'm thinking a lot bigger, planning a multi-million dollar business!

—**Daniel Morton, Nexus Fitness**

We invested $30k less than expected and attended two trade shows for which we have generated a combined 210 leads and over $135k-worth of work thus far, with $450k still alive in our pipeline that we expect to convert in the next 3 to 6 months. Our extreme follow up achieved these fantastic results.

—**Chris Chatfield, Chatfield AV**

We invested less than $1k in an amazing VIP night that has created over 30 leads which represents over $120k in potential sales.

—**Janelle Wareham, Interiors by Riveresque**

I just won a $500,000 contract, after almost giving up on my business.

—**Adam Wilson, Wilbart Pty Ltd**

My stress levels have gone from 9/10 to 4/10. I feel like I'm in control of something that's about to go BOOM!

—**Michael Karakolis, Fibonacci Stone**

Having Stefan as my business coach has been invaluable in reinvigorating me and my business. When I first met Stefan I was tired and in need of help to continually keep moving forward. Stefan's no-nonsense, down-to-earth approach helped me relate to him straight away. He manages to help me look at things differently and keeps me on track to continually stay focused on my business. Stefan helps me to see all the extraordinary things our business offers our customers and in our one-on-one meetings we work through where we are taking the business in the future.

With Stefan's encouragement I nominated my business for the Manningham Business Excellence Awards 2013. We won 'Contribution to Community' and were then thrilled to be announced as 'Manningham Business of the Year 2013'. I attribute so much of these Awards to Stefan's guidance and assurance.

—**Julie Quinton, Quinton's SUPA IGA**

Business is booming we are double what we were last year at this stage – more than DOUBLE! $420k in sales to-date this financial year, with still a week to go in September. We were at $201k end of September last year.

—**Tom Graham, Tough Glass Worx**

When I went to Stefan in December 2011 I was a small business owner with big dreams and vision but little know-how. Stefan taught me the fundamentals in business: discipline, delegation, cash flow, and most of all planning and clarity. I can highly recommend Stefan as the person who is going to give you the complete package to start you on your path to success. Don't be afraid, embrace the journey and grow!!

—**David Lindsay, Salts of the Earth**

Special people deserve special recognition and Stefan Kazakis and his Board of Directors 12 (BOD12) coaching program certainly fall into this category. I have been in Stefan's program for about seven months now and the success I have achieved is nothing short of a miracle.

Actually, it is not a miracle, it is Stefan's coaching that has enabled me to figure out some "blind spots" that I had. Stefan has the uncanny ability to put his finger on issues and provide distinctions just when they are needed. The learning environment that he has been able to create with his BOD12 program not only provides great resources and knowledge, but moreover, it provides a forum for coaching each other. Lots of learning is achieved on this level too, learning from each other.

The very refreshing difference between Stefan and other coaches (and I have had many and paid big money for some that provided questionable outcomes) is that Stefan has his heart and soul in enabling lasting progress and advancement in your business. In fact, Stefan goes out of his way to provide a forum for true business success. He is willing to connect people and resources, which shows the level of maturity that Stefan has elected to play on. Only serious business owners, "ones that truly wish to succeed and do the work" need apply…this is a brutal truth environment.

I can whole-heartedly recommend Stefan's BOD12 coaching program to ANY business owners that truly wish to advance themselves and their business to the next level, then to the next level, then to the next…

I am certain that I will be taking advantage of Stefan being on my team and that Stefan will still be coaching me for many more years to come, seeing that I am convinced that he is able to assist me in getting my knowledge and my business to many levels above where it is currently.

—Uwe Jacobs, Property Friends

I hired Stefan in October 2013 as a business coach. Since that time Stefan has instilled in me the business skills and confidence to launch new service-offerings and to grow the business.

Stefan has an infectious and charismatic demeanour. He's passionate about businesses succeeding, small businesses in particular, and this passion comes through in his coaching and his actions. Stefan's credentials and expertise as a business coach stem from his experience in saving and growing a family business. He understands business fundamentals as well as what it's like for a business to fail and to succeed. A further strength of Stefan's is that he understands any business; across market sectors. He understands the drivers and market pressures on a particular business and opportunities within any sector.

Stefan's clients are set apart from other small business owners with a single focus on a positive attitude and achieving business success. I would recommend Stefan to any business owner wishing to achieve these qualities.

—Deirdre Diamante, MIA Consulting Services

Our business has grown from the small home-based business model to an international organisation with the assistance of Stefan Kazakis. We are still using the services of Stefan two and a half years later and looking forward to more phenomenal growth to come. Stefan is an amazing business coach. The cost of not being coached might very well be the loss of your dream for your own business. Bite the bullet and call him today.

—Danielle Storey, Speaker, Mentor, Business Owner

If you want to create lasting and long-term changes in your company or business, there is NO better person in Australia that I can recommend than Stefan. He has revolutionised a number of my colleagues' companies in various fields of endeavour. He has a genuine, concentrated, professional approach. He is enthusiastic, passionate and is a great listener and speaker. He is on top of global financial trends and knows how to make recommendations to people, based upon his research and knowledge as a neo-entrepreneur. I have no hesitations in recommending him to anyone who wants to grow their business.

—**John Harris, Rewards Loyalty and Sales**

During the program we have increased our strategic market activity from 1 per week to 3 per week. This will equate to almost $1 million-worth of work in the next 12 months. Our average dollar sale has increased from $994 to $1,489 that's a 66% increase. Our profit result in the last 12 months has increased by 300%.

—**Brendan, The Drain Man**

During the program we have gone from $100k to $500k. We have gone from one van to three vans on the road and we now have an internal operations manager. Since I started on the program I have decreased my debt that I had accumulated over three years from $150k to almost paid off. That's due to understanding how to make profit. My stress levels have decreased from 10/10 to 5/10. I'm clear about the work ahead of me and what needs to be done. I understand the critical numbers in my business and the strategies to continue growing the important ones.

—**Glenn, Five Star Locksmiths**

In the context of group-based business learning, the sessions helped to grow and communicate common goals and inspiration to go on as a business and achieve results.

—**Prue Bretherton, Interiors by Riveresque**

Just to let you know we have achieved our accreditation to ISO9001. Your actions have made our company continue to manage better. Thanks for your work!

—**Brian Brandenburg, Chadoak Pty Ltd**

Stefan Kazakis can be contacted at:

Westfield Tower
Level 8, 619 Doncaster Road
Doncaster VIC 3108
(03) 9001 0878
www.deadwoodtodiamonds.com
www.stefankazakis.com